TEACHERS' NOTES

HOMES AROUND
THE WORLD

WAYLAND
photopacks

Albany Bilbe & Liz George

Edited by Globe Education, Nantwich, Cheshire
Designed by Pardoe Blacker Publishing, Lingfield, Surrey

First published in 1996 by Wayland Publishers Ltd
61 Western Road, Hove, East Sussex, BN3 1JD

**British Library Cataloguing-in-Publication Data
has been issued for this pack**

ISBN 0 7502 9003 X

This booklet is published as part of Wayland Photopacks
which contain 16 photocards. The booklet is not to be
sold separately.

Acknowledgements:
The authors gratefully acknowledge the following for
their comments quoted in the photopack: K. Rackham,
Stonemason, Norfolk (page 7); J. Jones, Gwent (page 7);
Mr Cross, Hanson Brick Company (page 10); Cassandra
Benjamin, Bricklayer (page 10); D. Wilton, (page 20);
Mr Comfrey, Narrowboat Owner (page 24); Eve,
Narrowboat Owner (page 24); Homeless Girl, London
(page 35); Fairground Showman, East Anglia (page 40).

The authors acknowledge the copyright holders for
permission to use the following extracts in the
photopack: From *A Century of Change: Homes* by
John Foster, Hodder & Stoughton, 1990 (page 15);
From *Going underground: houses with hidden depths* by
Crispin Aubrey, *Country Living* Magazine, January 1995
(page 17).

Although every attempt has been made to contact
copyright holders, the publishers have not been able to
contact everyone. We apologize for this apparent
negligence.

Picture agencies are acknowledged on the reverse of
the picture cards.
Cover picture: Alain Le Garsmeur/Impact.

Printed in Italy by G. Canale & C.S.p.A. –
Bogaro T.se – TURIN

CONTENTS

CURRICULUM ABBREVIATIONS:

POS = Programme of Study

SCIENCE
EIS   Experimental and Investigative Science
MP   Materials and their Properties
PP   Physical Properties
LPLT   Life Processes and Living Things

ENGLISH (ENG)
SL   Speaking and Listening
W   Writing

GEOGRAPHY (GEO)

MATHS
UAM   Using and Applying Mathematics
SSM   Shape, Space and Measure
N   Number
HD   Handling Data

PHYSICAL EDUCATION (PE)
GR   General Requirements

DESIGN AND TECHNOLOGY (D&T)

HISTORY (HIST)
KE   Key Elements
SU   Study Units

INTRODUCTION

We have selected the pictures for this photopack to explore housing through four key geographical themes. These are: availability of building materials; terrain and space; climate; and people's work. In addition, one photocard looks at the implications of building a modern house and another the significance of decoration. Discussion points and classroom activities are based on children's firsthand experience. This is to help them recognize the universal need for shelter, and relate their own housing needs to those of other people. The section, Potential of the Pack, demonstrates the flexibility of the photocards and suggests their use in exploring a wider range of themes than those already listed.

The photocards can be used on an individual, group or class basis. On the reverse of each card the text relates to the picture and gives additional information. Written on two levels, the bold text allows the younger and less experienced readers to extract key information that is further developed in the paragraphs.

We have employed appropriate and sometimes technical vocabulary so children become familiar with its use. We hope that the readers will find sufficient contextual clues to help with their understanding of less familiar words, and that the class discussions suggested reinforce their use and meaning.

The topic web provides an overall view of the activities covered within the curriculum. These activities are fully explained in the teachers' notes.

The teachers' notes for the study of *Homes Around the World* include background information, discussion points, detailed classroom activities and follow-up work designed to embrace key elements of the National

Curriculum Document 1995. Charts detail the areas of the National Curriculum covered by this pack.

Background notes provide geographical facts, historic development and current information linked with quotations from inhabitants and professionals. These are intended to support teachers in their preparation for this topic.

Discussion points aim to encourage children to reflect on their own experiences of housing as a means of appreciating the needs of people around the world. Discussion sessions should give everyone an opportunity to contribute, and become familiar with new vocabulary relating to the topic.

Classroom activities and follow-up work given for each photocard relate directly to the subject theme. Themes are explored through different areas of the curriculum to offer depth and breadth to children's understanding of the overall topic. They are written under curriculum headings.

The activity sheets have been designed to extend information on the photocards or in the teachers' notes, and allow children a chance to consolidate and demonstrate their knowledge and understanding. Selection by the teacher is necessary to match the activities to the ability of an individual child.

Book lists suggest titles for teacher reference. Information and fiction books suggested for children would broaden their experience of the topic by providing different viewpoints and situations relating to different types of housing.

Resources for the classroom and places to visit have been suggested.

TOPIC WEB

HOMES AROUND THE WORLD

SCIENCE
- Investigate how to make the best mortar
- Investigate different methods of insulation
- Investigate the strength of different building materials
- Look at trees
- Investigate a damp-proof course
- Test the strength of wall bonds
- Safety precautions at school and on a building site
- Use thermometers to measure temperature
- Investigate the strength of different structures
- Ways to join two pieces of wood
- Track the sun
- Make reinforced concrete
- Investigate tides
- The water cycle
- Solar energy
- Animals that live underground
- Animals that live near or in water

ENGLISH
- Word bonds
- Write a report about a visit
- Label displays
- Share writing a poem
- Write letters
- Present an oral report on an investigation
- Devise a housing questionnaire
- Role play living underground, homelessness, and being an estate agent

INFORMATION TECHNOLOGY
- Design a questionnaire
- Collate information

MUSIC
- Collect rhymes and songs relating to buildings
- Compose music to represent different weather conditions

ART
- Warm and cold colours
- Design patterns
- Wall rubbings
- Soap sculpture
- Decoration on buildings
- Close observational drawings to investigate wood
- Print a cityscape mural
- Look at the work of artists depicting housing
- Sketch the environment
- Weaving

HISTORY
- Investigate architectural periods
- Street names as a clue to the past
- Investigate the use of building materials in the past
- How people once decorated their homes
- Construct timelines
- Sheltering under the ground in the past

MATHEMATICS
- Measurement of time, length and temperature
- Tide-tables
- Capacity
- Angles
- Surveys
- Two-dimensional and three-dimensional shapes
- Use standard measures
- Tessellation
- Addition and multiplication
- Patterns and sequencing

GEOGRAPHY
- Weather conditions
- Rainfall
- Climate
- Caves
- Location of settlements
- Geographical features
- Types of rock
- Natural building materials
- Settlements
- Places
- Rivers
- Mountains
- Knowledge of own location
- Street surveys
- Giving and following directions
- Mapwork
- Using maps and globes
- Simple plans
- Environmental issues

DESIGN AND TECHNOLOGY
- Build a Lego model
- Design and make a variety of walls using different building materials
- Design and make a lift-the-flap book
- Make a working model of guttering
- Make a timber-framed house
- Investigate the function and suitability of different building materials
- Design and make a pulley system

5

CONTINENTS

HOMES IN EUROPE
1 Terraced cottages with stone roofs
9 Chalets are houses built in the mountains
14 The home of the British Prime Minister

HOMES IN AFRICA
2 A woman builds a brick house
4 Modern flats in Nairobi, Kenya
5 Caves are ready-made homes
11 Cairo is a hot, dry city in Egypt
13 Bedouin herdspeople live in tents
15 Lobi children decorate their homes

HOMES IN ASIA
6 In wet places, houses are built on stilts
7 Hong Kong has many tall buildings
8 Living and working on the River Li in China
12 A shanty town in Bombay, India

HOMES IN THE AMERICAS
3 Inuit live in the freezing north
10 A maloca in the rainforest

BUILDING MATERIALS

HOMES MADE OF STONE
1 Terraced cottages with stone roofs
5 Caves are ready-made homes

HOMES MADE OF WOOD OR PLANTS
3 Inuit live in the freezing north
6 In wet places, houses are built on stilts
9 Chalets are houses built in the mountains
10 A maloca in the rainforest

HOMES MADE OF CLAY OR BRICK
2 A woman builds a brick house
11 Cairo is a hot, dry city in Egypt
14 The home of the British Prime Minister
15 Lobi children decorate their homes
16 Modern houses save fuel

HOUSES MADE FROM
PRE-FABRICATED MATERIALS
3 Inuit live in the freezing north
4 Modern flats in Nairobi, Kenya
7 Hong Kong has many tall buildings
16 Modern houses save fuel

POTENTIAL OF THE PACK

CLIMATIC CONDITIONS

HOMES IN HOT PLACES
2 A woman builds a brick house
4 Modern flats in Nairobi, Kenya
5 Caves are ready-made homes
10 A maloca in the rainforest
11 Cairo is a hot, dry city in Egypt
12 A shanty town in Bombay, India
13 Bedouin herdspeople live in tents
15 Lobi children decorate their homes

HOMES IN COLD PLACES
3 Inuit live in the freezing north
9 Chalets are houses built in the mountains

HOMES IN WET PLACES
6 In wet places, houses are built on stilts
8 Living and working on the River Li in China
10 A maloca in the rainforest

LIFESTYLES

HOMES THAT GO WITH THE JOB
3 Inuit live in the freezing north
8 Living and working on the River Li in China
13 Bedouin herdspeople live in tents
14 The home of the British Prime Minister

HOMES OF THREATENED CULTURES
3 Inuit live in the freezing north
6 In wet places, houses are built on stilts
8 Living and working on the River Li in China
10 A maloca in the rainforest
13 Bedouin herdspeople live in tents

NOMADIC LIFESTYLE
3 Inuit live in the freezing north
10 A maloca in the rainforest
13 Bedouin herdspeople live in tents
12 A shanty town in Bombay, India

DECORATED HOMES
16 Lobi children decorate their homes

MULTI-STOREY HOMES
4 Modern flats in Nairobi, Kenya
7 Hong Kong has many tall buildings

HOMES BUILT TO CONSERVE ENERGY
3 Inuit live in the freezing north
9 Chalets are houses built in the mountains
16 Modern houses save fuel

Photocard numbers are shown in **bold** type

PHOTO

1

HOMES AROUND THE WORLD

TERRACED COTTAGES WITH STONE ROOFS

AREAS FOR STUDY

- Activities and fieldwork exploring the use of stone for building.
- An appreciation of the physical and human features influencing development and changes in local settlements.

SKILLS FOR GEOGRAPHY

- Observe and record similarities and differences between contrasting locations in Britain.
- Use appropriate geographical terms.
- Undertake local fieldwork.
- Use a variety of secondary sources to find geographical information.

BACKGROUND INFORMATION

Stone is an attractive and durable natural resource used for building throughout the world. Igneous rock, such as granite, is very hard and difficult to cut, and is mainly used in large slabs for bridges and curb stones. Sedimentary rocks, such as sandstone and limestone, are popular because they are easily cut and shaped. Metamorphic rock, such as slate (compressed clay) and marble (limestone changed by heat and pressure) are used for special purposes. Slate is easily split and is still sometimes used for roof tiles. Marble in Britain is used mainly for decoration, for example on fireplaces and steps.

Because the labour costs to extract and dress natural stone are high, reconstituted stone has become a popular alternative, but stonemasonry still survives as a skill. Stone is shaped and cut for decorative features, particularly for gravestones.

'Most of the stone is cut by machine, lettering is added using computer graphics and cut in by tungsten drill or grit blasting. But the traditional way is still used – by eye and hand-working with a hammer and chisel. Where decorative work, such as flowers or ears of corn, is needed then the main part of the stone is cut away by machine leaving a raised area, the details are then carved.'
K. RACKHAM, STONEMASON, NORFOLK

During the eighteenth and nineteenth centuries, many people moved from the country to work in factories in the towns. Terraced houses were quick and cheap to build. Building each house against the other saved on cost and space. The houses were constructed along short streets in rectangular blocks known as grid irons. Although they were mass-produced, their style still relied on local traditions and many early terraced houses were built from local stone in a cottage style.

'We live in an end-of-terrace house. We've always felt secure here, there's always someone close by to come to your aid, and of course you do get some warmth from the other house. But you never get much privacy out the back in the garden and the front door opens directly on to the pavement.'
J. JONES, GWENT

DISCUSSION POINTS

1. Ask children to describe their own homes. Include a house, a flat and a bungalow, taking into consideration their construction and style.
- Where is it built?
- Why do they think that site was chosen?
- Is the whole street the same type of housing, such as terraced?
- Have the same materials been used for all the housing in the street?

2. Consider why people need shelter.
- Discuss the features that all homes have in common, such as walls, roof and entrance.
- Are the building materials used in children's homes local, manufactured or natural?
- Discuss children's experience of terraced housing. Compare the terraced cottage-style on the photocard with modern town houses.

CLASSROOM ACTIVITIES

ART K.S.1: 1, 2B, 4D, 5A,B, 7A, 8A, 9A,B,C,E; K.S.2: 1, 2B, 4D, 5A,B, 7A, 8A, 9A,B,C,D,E. Make rubbings or drawings of local stone walls. How does the finish of the stone differ? Compare the finish of a step with the finish of a window lintel. Why isn't all stone finished in the same way?

7

SCIENCE K.S.1: POS 1B, 2A, 4A,B, 5A,B; EIS 1A,B,C, 2B,C, 3A,C,D,E,F; MP 1A,C,E; K.S.2: POS 1B, 2B, 3A, 4A,C, 5A,B; EIS 1A,B,C,D, 2B, 3B,C,D,E,.; MP 1A. ENG K.S.1&2: W 1A,B,C.

Collect a range of different stones (such as slate, granite, or sandstone) and devise a test (for example a scratch test) to find out which is the hardest. Make notes about what happened for each stone. Display the stones in order of hardness and label each with your findings.

SCIENCE K.S.1: POS 1B, 2A, 4A,B, 5A,B; MP 1C,E; K.S.2: POS 1B, 2B, 3A, 4A,C, 5A,B, MP 1A. D&T K.S.1: 1B, 2B,C, 3C,F, 4C,E,F, 5B,F; K.S.2: 1B, 2A,C, 3D,F,G, 4C,F,G, 5B,E,J.

Collect small stones with which to build a dry stone wall. Put the stones one on top of the other with no mortar between. What must you consider to make the wall stable? Wearing a face mask and gloves for protection, investigate with different proportions of sand, cement and water to find the most effective 'mortar' for sticking your stones together to form a wall.

MATHS KS1: UAM 1A,B, 2D, 3A; N 1C; SSM 2A,B,C; K.S.2: SSM 1E, 3C.

Make the tallest wall you can with wooden bricks. Which shapes are most stable? How high and how wide is your wall? Is it straight and level? Use a plumb-line and spirit-level to check. Check other walls around the school.

ART K.S.1: 1, 2C, 4A,D, 6, 7C, 8B,D,E, 9B,C; K.S.2: 1, 2C, 4A,D, 5A,B, 6, 7C,E, 8A,C,E, 9A,B,C.

Masons shape stone with a hammer and chisel. Use clay modelling tools and kitchen knives to model a block of hard soap. Consider how to achieve a smooth or rough finish. How might you need to adapt your tools?

ENG K.S.1: W 1A,B,C; K.S.2: W 1A,B,C. D&T K.S.1: 1A,B, 2B, 3A,B, 4A,B, 5G; K.S.2: 1A,B, 2B,C, 3A,B,F,G, 4A,B,C, F,G, 5K.

Using a book as a stimulus, for example Jan Pienowski's *Haunted House*, design and make a lift-the-flap book to describe your own home. Use appropriate vocabulary for describing specific structural features.

FOLLOW-UP WORK

GEO K.S.1: 1C, 3F; K.S.2: 1A, 3E, 4, 5A,C, 9C, 10A.

Study stone buildings, such as the Great Wall of China or the Tower of London. What stone was used?

SCIENCE K.S.1: POS 1B, 2A; EIS 1A; MP 1A,B,C; K.S.2: POS 1B; EIS 1A; MP 1A,D, 3A.

Dig earth from your school garden. Separate the stones from the soil and wash them. Can you identify the type of rock you have found? Is it local stone, or has it been dumped there by builders?

ART K.S.1& 2: 1, 2B, 5A,B, 7A, 8A, 9A,B,C,D,E; HIST K.S.1: AOS 1A,B; KE 1B, 2C, 4A; K.S.2: 1B, 2A,B, 4A.

Survey the use of stone in a local street. Where has the stone come from? What are the functions of these buildings? Do you think they were built by rich or poor people? Find out when they were built?

HIST K.S.1: 1A,B; KE 4A; K.S.2: 4A.

Do any street names in your district give clues as to when or why buildings were erected? Look at old terraced housing. Comment on modernization through pictures and notes.

BOOKS FOR THE CLASSROOM

POINTERS: THE STORY OF THE CASTLE
by Miriam Moss (Macdonald Young Books 1993)
Fascinating facts about castles and fortified homes.

A CENTURY OF CHANGE: HOMES
by John Foster (Hodder and Stoughton 1990)
Looks at changes in homes.

OUR HOUSE
by Emma and Paul Rogers (Walker 1991)
This delightful picture book demonstrates the building of a stone house, and how subsequent occupants have altered it over time.

USING ACTIVITY SHEET NO: 1

A folded paper house to construct. Glue and scissors are not required. Completed, it can be used to display written or pictorial information.

FOLDING A PAPER HOUSE

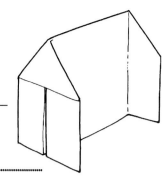

ACTIVITY SHEET 1

Name... Class..

■ Use this sheet or an A4 piece of paper.

1. Fold the paper in half (fold A).

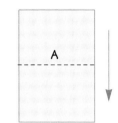

2. Fold it in half along (fold B) to crease the paper. Open out again.

3. Fold the edges into the centre to crease the paper and open out (folds C and D) again.

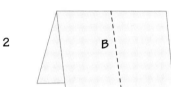

4. Fold down the corners E and F to crease into triangles. Open out again.

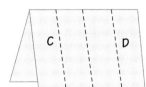

5. Open apart ends X and Y to meet at the centre fold B and flatten triangles E and F.

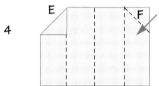

6. Now fold back both ends so they are at right angles to the paper and the model will stand upright to make a house shape.

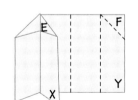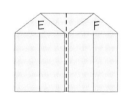

7. Decorate to make it look like a row of terraced cottages.

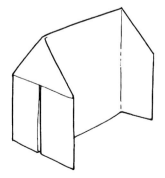

WAYLAND PUBLISHERS LTD, 61 WESTERN ROAD, HOVE, EAST SUSSEX BN3 1JD

PHOTO

2

H O M E S   A R O U N D   T H E   W O R L D

A WOMAN BUILDS A BRICK HOUSE

AREAS FOR STUDY

- To explore types of brick used for building.
- An appreciation of physical and human features influencing development and changes in settlements.

SKILLS FOR GEOGRAPHY

- Observe and record similarities and differences between Britain and Africa.
- Use appropriate geographical terms.
- Undertake local fieldwork.
- Use a variety of secondary sources to find geographical information.

BACKGROUND INFORMATION

Bricks have been used for thousands of years and are probably still the most common building material. The photocard shows a member of a co-operative in Namibia building a house. Across the developing world, the provision of housing is a growing problem and people are encouraged to build for themselves, but it takes time. Simple, hand-pressing machines allow building blocks to be made by mixing water and a little cement with soil. This is a cheap building material that can be produced at or near the building site. British bricks are mostly machine-made to a standard size and fired at a temperature of 1,000 °C to make them resilient to water and frost. The chemical content of the clay used dictates the final colour of the bricks.

'There are about 100 different types of clay but only about twelve are used in brick-making. At Hanson Brick, we would use all kinds as we are based all over the country. For example, at what was formerly London Brick, which has been going for over 100 years, Lower Oxford clay is used; at Butterly, which has been going for about 200 years, they use Cooper Marl.'
MR CROSS, HANSON BRICK COMPANY

Bricks are laid in courses and the vertical joints are off-set to prevent weakness in the wall. The pattern made is called the 'bond'. Lengthways bricks are 'stretchers'; end-on bricks are 'headers'.

'I saw an advert for trainee bricklayers and labourers and got accepted. I was very good at labouring so they put me on a trainee bricklaying course for two months. Bricklaying is a really skilled job and there are not many really good bricklayers. I came joint-top out of fifteen others (all men). From there, I applied for an apprenticeship. Before bricklaying, I was a nurse so I was used to lifting people, so it was no problem carrying sacks of cement or hods of bricks.'
CASSANDRA BENJAMIN, BRICKLAYER

Only a few courses of bricks can be laid at one time as the wall distorts under its own weight. Bricklayers use a plumb-line and a spirit-level to check that the courses are vertical and level.

DISCUSSION POINTS

1. Discuss parts of the school or children's homes constructed from brick.
- Are they all the same colour?
- Where in the building are they used?

2. The availability of clay makes brick a common resource in much of the world. Do the children know where clay comes from?
- Why are bricks a low cost resource?
- What tools and materials are used for bricklaying?

3. Discuss with children social stereotyping and the role women have as builders.
- What other building work will the Namibian building co-operative need to tackle?
- Discuss the shape and type of roof, and size of windows suitable for a hot country.

CLASSROOM ACTIVITIES

SCIENCE K.S.1: In wet countries, brick walls must
POS 1A,B, 2A, 3; be protected from moisture rising
EIS 1A,B,C, 2B,C, up them from the ground. When
3A,C,D,E,F; MP several courses of bricks have been
1A,C; K.S.2: 1A,B, laid, the builder puts in a damp-
2A,B, 3A, 4A; EIS proof course, which is often made
1A,B,D, 2B,C, from a layer of waterproof tarred
3B,C,D,E; MP 1A. felt. Investigate how this works.

MATHS K.S.1: Investigate the surfaces and edges of a cuboid. Are all the faces the same size? Using a range of bricks, investigate shapes that tessellate, and those most suitable for building walls. Record your findings.

MATHS K.S.1 references: UAM 1A; SSM 1A,C, 2A,B,C; K.S.2: UAM 1A,B,C, 3A; SSM 1A, 1A,B.

MATHS K.S.1: One hod carries twenty bricks. How many journeys would the hod carrier make to build a wall of 200 bricks? A wall is twenty bricks high and 500 bricks long. How many bricks are needed? Invent similar problems.

MATHS K.S.1 references: UAM 1A, 2A,C,D, 3A; N 1C,D, 2A,B, 4A,B,C; K.S.2: UAM 1A,B,C, 2B, C,D, 3A; N 1A,2A, 3A,C,D,E,F, 4B.

ENG K.S.1: R 2B. Devise a 'brick wall' of word bonds, verb endings or root words such as 'car – pet' or 'build - ing'.

ART K.S.1&2: 1, 2B,C, 4A, 5A,B, 6, 7A,C,E,F, 8A,B,D, 9,A,B,C,D,E; Take wax rubbings from a variety of brick walls. Paint a wash over them to reveal the bonds. Which is the most commonly used bond?

SCIENCE POS 1A,B, 2A, 3; EIS 1A,B,C, 2B,C, 3A,C,D,E,F; PP 2B,C,D; K.S.2: 1A,B, 2A,B, 3A, 4A; EIS 1A,B,D. 2B,C, 3B,C,D,E; PP 2G,H. Using different construction materials (for example small sweet boxes) build walls using different bonds. Develop a variety of investigations to test their strength. Record your investigation and the results.

ENG K.S.1: W 1A,B,C; K.S.2: W 1A,B,C, 2D. Write a new version of the poem, *This is the House that Jack built,* using technical building terms.

FOLLOW-UP WORK

SCIENCE K.S.1: POS 1B, 2A, 4A,B; EIS 2A,B,C, 3A,B,C,F; MP 1A,B,E; K.S.2: POS 1B, 2A,B, 3A, 4A,C; EIS 2A,B,C, 2B,C, 3A,B,C,E; MP 1A. Make a collection of different bricks, such as perforated air bricks, engineering bricks, or breeze blocks. Make a detailed chart to recording size, colour, texture and particular such as frogs, or holes. Find out which part of a building they are used for.

ENG K.S.1: W 1A,B,C; K.S.2: W 1A,B,C. Visit a building site to find out how bricks are laid. At school write a report on bricklaying.

ENG K.S.1&2: W 1A,B,C. Make and label a descriptive display of tools for bricklaying.

SCIENCE K.S.1&2: POS 2A, 5A,B. Make the imaginative play area into a building site. Make tools, safety helmets and warning posters.

MUSIC K.S.1: 4B,5A. Collect rhymes and songs such as *London Bridge Is Falling Down.*

RESOURCES FOR THE CLASSROOM

WOMEN'S EDUCATION IN BUILDING
London W10 5UP. Tel 0181 964 0255.
Trains women for the building trade.

HANSON BRICK COMPANY
Bedford, MK43 9LZ. Tel 0733 350035.
Has information on brick-making.

BOOKS FOR THE CLASSROOM

LINKS: BRICKS
by Graham Rickard (Wayland 1991)
An information book for top infants upwards.

WHO'S AFRAID OF THE BIG BAD WOLF
by Tony Bradman and Margaret Chamberlain
(Little Mammoth 1989)
Humorous story with girl pig building a house.

THE TRUE STORY OF THE THREE LITTLE PIGS
by Jon Scieszka (Puffin 1991)

MISS BRICK THE BUILDER'S BABY
by Allan Ahlberg and Colin McNaughton (Puffin 1989)

USING THE ACTIVITY SHEET NO: 2

A number operations activity for exploring and predicting number patterns. It can be tackled at different levels by varying the operation to subtractions, multiplication or division.

NUMBERING WALLS

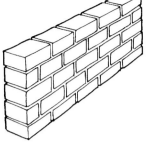

ACTIVITY SHEET 2

Name.. Class..

Look at this example:

Add 2	3	5	7	9	11	
Add 5	3	8	13	18	23	28
Add 10	3	13	23	33	43	
Add 11	3	14	25	36	47	58

1. Start with the number 3 in the top left hand brick. Add 2 for each brick along the top row and write the sum on to each brick.

2. Complete the wall a row at a time, starting with 3 and adding the number marked alongside the row.

■ Are there any rows with all even numbers?

■ Are there any rows with all odd numbers?

■ Which rows have mixed odd and even numbers?

■ What would happen if you carried on laying 4 more bricks on each course?

■ Can you find any patterns for each course?

Now make up your own walls.

■ Start with 5.

Add 2
Add 5
Add 10
Add 11

■ Start with ......

Add .....
Add .....
Add .....
Add .....

■ Start with ......

Add .....
Add .....
Add .....
Add .....

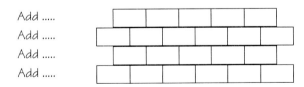

■ Start with ......

Add .....
Add .....
Add .....
Add .....

■ Start with ......

Add .....
Add .....
Add .....
Add .....

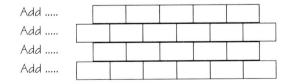

■ Start with ......

Add .....
Add .....
Add .....
Add .....

WAYLAND PUBLISHERS LTD, 61 WESTERN ROAD, HOVE, EAST SUSSEX BN3 1JD

PHOTO

3

HOMES AROUND THE WORLD

INUIT LIVE IN THE FREEZING NORTH

AREAS FOR STUDY

- To develop an understanding of how and why communities of people are changing.
- To investigate the theme of building materials in their own location and in a wider geographical context, for example wood.
- Classroom activities and fieldwork exploring questions such as, 'Why is wood used for building?'
- An appreciation of the physical and human features influencing the development and changes in their location.
- How and why settlements evolve in a particular way.
- An ability to recognize patterns of settlement development in relation to availability of resources and human needs.

SKILLS FOR GEOGRAPHY

- Focus on the locality of school and contrast findings with an Inuit settlement.
- Observe and record similarities and differences between locations.
- Use appropriate geographical terms.
- Undertake local fieldwork looking at prefabricated and wooden buildings.
- Use a variety of secondary sources to find geographical information.
- Develop an appreciation of seasonal changes in temperature.
- Consider the effects of climate on the way people live.

BACKGROUND NOTES

For thousands of years Inuit have lived along the coastal areas of Greenland, Arctic North America and north-east Siberia. They adapted to the harsh climate surviving on the many animals and fish. In winter, they dug homes below ground, sometimes using whale bones insulated by animal skins for rafters. In the summer they camped on the ice in skin tents. Occasionally when hunting, they made temporary shelters of blocks of snow called illuviga (not igloo, that just means house). During the 1950s many Inuit worked as labourers building early-warning stations for the USA and USSR. They lived in labourers' camps which later developed into the Inuit settlements of today. The wooden houses have small and low rooms which are easily heated. They were mostly imported in kit form. Wood is warm, strong and light, and when treated with preservatives is very durable. Much of the wood comes from faraway renewable forests, for example in Canada. The timber is seasoned to remove water that can be up to half the total weight. It becomes less prone to decay, and lighter to handle. It can be air-dried, which takes several months, or kiln-dried, which takes days. Both methods require careful handling to prevent the wood from warping. Only seasoned timber is used for construction.

In Britain, prefabricated homes are not a new idea. In Tudor London, timber-framed structures were imported from the Weald and Essex. After the Second World War, numerous prefabricated homes were erected to solve the acute housing shortage. These were designed to last for only ten years, but some are still in use today.

DISCUSSION POINTS

1. How do we describe the temperature outside?
- Discuss the children's experience of changing seasons and how it compares to an Inuit's experience.
- Discuss how the number of hours of daylight changes with the season. Compare Britain to Arctic regions where the sun never sets in mid-summer and never rises in mid-winter.

2. How do children keep warm in cold weather? How are their homes heated and insulated?
- Discuss how they think insulation works.
- Which parts of children's own homes are made of wood? Why do they think it has been used for that particular function?

3. Discuss how timber frameworks are factory assembled, for ease of construction at the building site.
- Do children recognize any kit-built houses or prefabricated buildings in their locality?
- Discuss the importance of renewable forests for building construction.

CLASSROOM ACTIVITIES

SCIENCE K.S.1: POS 1B, 2A,B,C, 3, 4A,B; EIS 1A,B, 2A,B,C, 3A,B,C,D, E,F; K.S.2: 1B, 2A,B,C,D, 3B, 4A,B,C; EIS 1A,B, 2A,B,C, 3B,C,D,E. IT K.S.1: POS 1A, 2A,B,C; K.S.2: POS 1B,C, 2A,B, C,D.

An outdoor thermometer will keep a record of the temperature outside your school. Use it to help you describe the weather conditions. At 0 °C water freezes, at 20 °C it is warm and at 40 °C it is hot. Are there variations in the temperature at different times of the day? Make records in the early morning, at midday and in late afternoon. What are the variations over the seasons? Collate your information using a computer.

D&T K.S.1: 1B, 2A,C, 3C,F, 5B; K.S.2: 1B, 2A,C, 3F,G, 4F, 5E.

Using construction kits or straws, make a variety of frameworks for a house. Devise tests to find the strongest structure.

The next activity must be supervised.

D&T K.S.1: 1A,B, 2A, 4A,B,C,F, 5B,F,G; K.S.2: 1A,B, 2A, 4A,B,C,F,G, 5B,E,J.

Make a timber-framed Inuit house. You will need; lengths of 1 cm² wood, a bench block, a hacksaw, thin card, PVA glue, and scissors.
1. Draw sixteen 3 cm squares on card. Draw a line diagonally across each. Cut the triangles.
2. Cut four 50 cm pieces of wood and eight 25 cm pieces of wood.
3. Make two wooden rectangles securing each corner on both sides with glue and the card triangles. Leave to dry.
4. Using the same method, join the rectangles together to form a cuboid box.
Consider the best materials for cladding the walls and roof.

ART K.S.1&2: 1, 2B, 4A,D, 5A,B, 7A,B, 8A,B,C,D, 9A.

Draw examples of the use of wood in buildings. Sketch the structure and types of joints used, such as door frame.Make drawings of wood to highlight knots and patterns of the grain.

SCIENCE K.S.1&2: POS 1A,B, 2A, 3, 4B; EIS 1A,B,C 2A,B,C,D,E.

How many ways can you find to join two pieces of wood? Devise tests to investigate their strength.

HIST K.S.1&2: AOS 1A,B; KE 1A,B, 4A, 5.

How was wood used in the past for building houses? Make labelled drawings and put them in chronological order.

FOLLOW-UP WORK

SCIENCE K.S.1&2: POS 1B, 2A, MP 1A,B,C,D,E.

Make a display of wooden objects. Try to identify the different types of wood.

SCIENCE K.S.1&2: POS 1B, 2B, 4B; EIS 1A,B, 2B,C, 3A,B,C,D,F; PP 1A,B.

Use reference points such as a tree or a building to track the sun's position in the sky. Make comparisons over the year.

ENG K.S.1: W 1A,B,C; K.S.2: W 1A,B,C.

Write to a meteorological office for information about daylight hours.

BOOKS FOR THE CLASSROOM

THREATENED CULTURES: INUIT
by Bryan and Cherry Alexander (Wayland 1992)

WHAT DO WE KNOW ABOUT THE INUIT
by Bryan and Cherry Alexander (Macdonald Young Books 1995)

HOUSES OF SNOW, SKIN AND BONE
by Bonnie Shemie (Tundra 1996)

THE VISUAL DICTIONARY OF BUILDINGS
(Dorling Kindersley 1992)
An illustrated dictionary of buildings.

FIND OUT ABOUT WOOD
by Henry Pluckrose (Watts 1994)
A series covering a range of materials including *WOOD, CLAY,* and *ROCK AND STONE.*

PHOTO
4
HOMES AROUND THE WORLD

MODERN FLATS IN NAIROBI, KENYA

AREAS FOR STUDY

- To develop an understanding of how and why communities of people are changing.
- To investigate the theme of building materials such as wood, locally and in a wider geographical context.
- Classroom activities and fieldwork exploring questions such as, Why and where are prefabricated materials used for building?
- An appreciation of the physical and human features influencing the development and changes in their own and other locations.
- How and why settlements evolve in a particular way.
- An ability to recognize patterns of settlement development in relation to availability of resources and human needs.

SKILLS FOR GEOGRAPHY

- Focus on the locality of the school and contrast findings with Nairobi, Kenya.
- Observe and record similarities in city life throughout the world.
- Consider the influence of economic activity on the size and development of a settlement.
- Use appropriate geographical terms.
- Undertake local fieldwork looking at prefabricated and wooden buildings.
- Use a variety of secondary sources to find geographical information.

BACKGROUND NOTES

After the Second World War, many cities were rebuilt using new techniques which revolutionized the construction industry. Components could be mass-produced in factories using concrete, ready for assembly on-site. Concrete, made by mixing cement, aggregate (such as crushed stone) and water, had steel rods inserted before it hardened, increasing its strength and flexibility. High-rise building became a symbol of modern post-war thinking, but many people could not adapt to high-rise living and some of the first tower blocks built in Europe in the 1950s and 1960s have now been replaced with more conventional houses and gardens.

'One day I stepped into the lifts at the flats. The doors closed but I was too small to reach the button. I stood there, in tears, terrified, until my dad found me. I never entered the lifts again.'
FROM A CENTURY OF CHANGE: HOMES BY JOHN FOSTER

In the developing countries of Africa and Asia, high-rise building is a solution for inner-city housing problems, and is increasing in popularity. Nairobi has an estimated population of well over one million, rising yearly. Many people are housed in high-rise buildings. These are quick and cheap to construct and provide a more modern standard of living than conventional housing. Safety is of paramount importance with so many people living together in the same building. Fire-resistant materials are used, smoke detectors and sprinklers are integral to the structure as well as fire doors and emergency exits.

DISCUSSION POINTS

1. Ask the children who live in flats to describe what they like and what they dislike about high-rise living.
• What do the other children think would be the advantages and disadvantages?

2. What do the children understand about cement and concrete?
• Discuss the differences between manufactured and natural building materials.
• Look around the classroom. Ask children to comment on its construction. Is there any evidence of manufactured or natural materials?
• Ask children to comment on the use of manufactured materials in their homes, such as double-glazed windows.

3. Discuss with the children their nearest city.
• Is there a mixture of old and new properties?
• Are there many high-rise properties?
• Are houses, flats and offices sited together or separately?
• Are the shops in one area, or are they spread around the city?
• Could they easily walk from one side of the city to the other?

15

CLASSROOM ACTIVITIES

D&T K.S.1: 1C, 5D,E; **K.S.2:** 1C, 5G,H,I,J.

Survey the use of manufactured building materials in your school. Where are they used? Why were they chosen? Do you prefer natural or manufactured products?

SCIENCE K.S.1: POS 1A,B, 2A,B, 4A,B, 5A,B; **EIS** 1A,B,C 2B,C, 3A,B,C,D,E,F; **MP** 1A, 2A; **K.S.2: POS** 1A,B, 2A,B, 4A,C, 5A,B; **EIS** 1A,B,C,D, 2B,C, 3A,B,C,D,E. **IT K.S.1:** 1A, 2A,B,C; **K.S.2:** 1B,C, 2A,B,C.

Investigate which proportions of sand, cement, gravel and water make the strongest concrete. Wear a face mask to keep out the cement dust and rubber gloves to protect your hands. Make up different mixes and pour into Vaseline-greased yoghurt pots or paint palettes. Predict which mix you think will be the best. Record your mixes and the results of your findings using a computer.

SCIENCE K.S.1: POS 1A,B, 2A,B, 4A,B, 5A,B; **EIS** 1A,B,C 2B,C, 3A,B,C,D,E,F; **MP** 1A, 2A; **K.S.2: POS** 1A,B, 2A,B, 4A,C, 5A,B; **EIS** 1A,B,C,D, 2B,C, 3A,B,C,D,E. **D&T K.S.1:** 1A,B, 2A,B,C, 4C,F, 5B,D,E,F; **K.S.2:** 1A,B, 2A,B,C, 4A,B,C, 5B,E,G,I,J.

Investigate the difference between concrete and reinforced concrete by building two bridges, reinforcing one with wire. You will need sand, cement, gravel, tap water, two Swiss roll tins lined with plastic smeared with Vaseline, eight small yoghurt pots greased with Vaseline, a bucket, a wire coat hanger, wire cutters, water, rubber gloves, and a trowel.

1. Cut three pieces of wire to fit lengthways into one tin and eight lengths to fit in four pots.
2. Mix concrete. Use three parts gravel, two parts sand, and one part cement. Stir in water until the mixture is stiff.
3. Half fill one tin with concrete. Lay wire on top and cover with concrete. Fill the other tin, leaving out the wire.
4. Fill all the pots with concrete and insert two strips of wire into four of them.
5. Leave the concrete to harden.
6. Remove the moulds.
7. Build two bridges: one without wire and one with. Use the pot blocks as uprights and lay the slabs across the top.
8. Devise methods for testing the strength of each bridge.
9. Observe and record your results.

ENG K.S.1: SL 1A,B,C, 2A,B, 3A; **K.S.2: SL** 1A,B,C, 2A,B, 3A. **D&T K.S.1:** 1A,B, 2A,B,C, 3A,B,C,D, E,F, 4C,F, 5B,D,E, F,G; **K.S.2:** 1A,B, 2A,B,C, 3B,C,D, F,G, 4C,E,F,G, 5E,G,H,I.

In groups, build tower blocks using plastic straws and Sellotape. Allow fifteen minutes for the task. Within your group discuss the success of your building and issues such as the strengths and properties of different shapes, structures, methods of construction, distribution of tasks, and teamwork. Prepare a presentation to explain your design to other groups.

ART K.S.1: 1, 2C, 4D, 7C,D, 8C,D,E,F; **K.S.2:** 1, 2C, 4D, 7C,D, 8C,D,E,F.

Look at modern paintings of cityscapes. Draw a modern city skyline to use as a mural. Print with sponges, rollers and a variety of junk materials to produce different silhouettes and textures.

ART K.S.1: 1, 2C, 4D, 7C,D, 8C,D,E,F; **K.S.2:** 1, 2C, 4D, 7C,D, 8C,D,E,F.

Make a city skyline silhouette-picture. Use marbling ink to make a background sky and glue a range of buildings cut from black paper into position to make a skyline.

FOLLOW-UP WORK

ENG K.S.1: SL 1A,B,C, 2A,B, 3A; **W** 1A,B,C; **K.S.2: SL** 1A,B,C, 2A,B, 3A; **W** 1A,B,C.

Visit a builders' merchant and look at different home building materials, including plastics and metals. Find out where they are manufactured. Talk to the manager about how goods arrive at the yard. Find out how tall buildings are constructed. For example, the types of machinery used to lift building materials up high-rise structures, or how a lift shaft is assembled.

PHOTO 5

HOMES AROUND THE WORLD

CAVES ARE READY-MADE HOMES

AREAS FOR STUDY

- An appreciation of the physical and human features influencing the development and changes in the environment.
- To investigate the influence of the physical terrain and the availability of building space, on where people make their homes.
- Classroom activities and fieldwork exploring questions such as, 'What is life like in a cave?'
- How and why settlements evolve in a particular way.
- An ability to recognize patterns of settlement development in relation to availability of resources, economic activity and human needs.

SKILLS FOR GEOGRAPHY

- Undertake local fieldwork looking at conditions underground or in areas well-shaded from the sun.
- Focus on the locality of school and contrast with living conditions of Tunisian caves.
- Look at weather conditions affecting how and where people live.
- Consider how site conditions influence the weather.
- Look at the physical features of a place that make it a desirable settlement, such as access to grazing land and natural shelter.
- Think about how features of a locality, such as grazing land, influence human activity.
- Use appropriate geographical terms.
- Use a variety of secondary sources to find geographical information.

BACKGROUND NOTES

Over thousands of years running water or blowing sand wear away exposed rock, sometimes forming caves. In limestone areas, rainwater absorbs carbon dioxide and acids from the soil. As it soaks down through the limestone below, it gradually dissolves away the rock, forming chambers. Where a river is flowing through a gorge, the action of the passing water quarries and excavates the river-bed, forming underwater caves. As the gorge becomes deeper, the level of the water drops and the caves are exposed in the sides of the gorge. In desert or semi-desert areas, wind-bourne sand scours away at out-crops of rock and cliff faces. Over time caves form in the rock.

Cave dwelling dates back to the Stone Age, about two million years ago. Caves were probably used by nomadic hunters as seasonal camps as they followed herds of animals. Archaeologists have been able to create a good picture of their lives from the finds inside caves. Dry caves contain moistureless air which restricts bacterial decay thus preserving bones, artefacts and paintings.

People still live in caves today. In Tunisia, the caves at Matmata are still inhabited by Berber sheep farmers. In Australia a large community lives in disused mining tunnels in Coober Pedy. In the last twenty years, over 6,000 underground homes have been built in North America. In Britain, there are very few cave dwellings, but one home is *The Sett* in Herefordshire.

'The house has been built into the remains of a thirteenth-century quarry. Major structural engineering was required to support the roof and maintain a barrier against water that flows down the hillside. You can walk right round the house through an underground passageway designed to keep damp out and lined with the giant, flat stones of the original quarry wall. Part of the quarry has been kept as a wine cellar. The roof itself has successive layers of insulation, concrete, felt, flagstones and earth. To maximize light, the south-west facing frontage is a forty-foot strip of French windows... bedrooms open off a circular central area with a large, domed roof light. Smaller roof windows let light into the other rooms.'
Country Living Magazine, January 1995

DISCUSSION POINTS

1. Discuss factors, such as climate, which may be reasons preventing more people in Britain from living in caves.
- What other natural shelters can the children think of that people could use?
- Discuss being underground in subways, car parks, and basement flats. Encourage children to comment on the availability of natural light and fresh air.

2. Ask children who have visited caves to describe their experiences. Would they consider caves to be suitable as homes.

• Discuss comparisons between the caves they have visited and those in the photograph on the photocard.

• Discuss the type of landscape where caves are often found, and why these caves would be a practical housing solution for shepherds.

CLASSROOM ACTIVITIES

ART K.S.1: 1, 2c, 4d, 7c,d, 8c,d,e,f; **K.S.2:** 1, 2c, 4d, 7c,d, 8c,d,e,f.

Carve caves in a soft brick. Consider how people would reach a cave that was part way up a cliff. In a hot climate, what would you do about fresh air in a cave?

SCIENCE K.S.1: POS 1b, 2a,b, 3, 4a; EIS 1a,b, 2a,b,c, 3a,c,d, e,f; **K.S.2:** 1b, 2a,b,c,d, 3b, 4a,b,c; EIS 1a,b, 2a,b,c, 3b,c,d,e. **MATHS K.S.1:** UAM 1a, 2,b,d; SSM 1a,c, 4b; **K.S.2:** UAM 1a,b,c, 2a, 3a; SSM 1e, 4b.

Where would be the coolest part of the cave for storing food? Using a room thermometer, check and record the temperature of the rooms in different parts of your school. What influences their temperature?

D&T K.S.1: 1a,b, 2a,b, 3a,b,c,d,e,f, 4a,b,c,e,f, 5a,b, d,e,f,g; **K.S.2:** 1a,b, 2a,b,c, 3a,b,c,d,f,g, 4a,b,c,e,f,g, 5a,c,e,g,h,i.

Imagine you live in an upper-storey cave which you need to furnish. Design and make a pulley system for raising heavy pieces of furniture.

SCIENCE K.S.1: POS 1c; **LPLT** 5a,b; **K.S.2:** POS 1c; **LPLT** 1a,b.

Many animals live underground for much of their time. List as many as you can. How have they adapted to life underground?

HIST K.S.1: POS 1b; KE 3a, 4a; **K.S.2:** KE 1b, 4a. **ART K.S.1:** 1, 2b,c, 3, 5b, 7a,b,c,d, 8b,e, 9a; **K.S.2:** 1, 2b,c, 3, 5b, 7a,b,c,d, 8b,e, 9a.

Research some early cave paintings. How did prehistoric people decorate the inside of their caves? Do the paintings tell you anything about their lifestyle? How would you decorate the inside of your cave? Design a large wall painting that would inform people in the future of how you live today.

HIST K.S.1: POS 1a, KE 2b,c, 4a; **K.S.2:** 2a, 4a.

During air-raids in the Second World War many people took shelter in shop basements, church crypts, the London Underground and caves. Find out how people entertained themselves during an air-raid.

FOLLOW-UP WORK

ENG K.S.1: SL 1a,b,c,d, 2a,b; **K.S.2:** SL 1a,b,c,d, 2a,b.

Visit local caves or a local subway. Describe your experiences. Use discussions to develop role play for situations of living underground.

ENG K.S.1: SL 1c, 2a,b; **K.S.2:** SL 1c, 2a,b.

Invite a pot-holer or someone who works underground to come and share their experiences. How do they compare with your own experiences?

USING THE ACTIVITY SHEET NO: 3

A colony of ants live in a maze of underground tunnels. There are a variety of ways they can reach the surface. Children are asked to work out what they think would be the shortest route, then to write down this route using simple and clear geographic directions.

AN UNDERGROUND ANT COLONY

ACTIVITY SHEET 3

Name.. Class..

Find out how the ants get through the mazes of underground tunnels to reach the surface.

■ Can you find more than one route? Use coloured pencils to try out different routes.

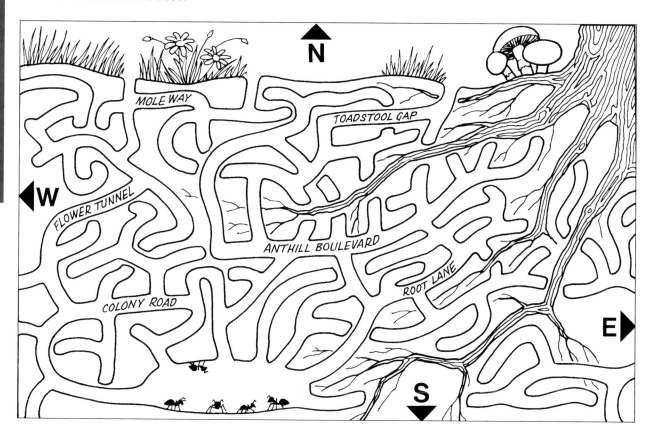

■ Decide on the shortest route and write clear instructions for others to follow. You can use compass directions, landmarks, and right and left turns. State where to start and name the tunnel where you come out.

Start at:

Come out at:

WAYLAND PUBLISHERS LTD, 61 WESTERN ROAD, HOVE, EAST SUSSEX BN3 1JD

PHOTO

6

HOMES AROUND THE WORLD

IN WET PLACES, HOUSES ARE BUILT ON STILTS

AREAS FOR STUDY

- An appreciation of the physical and human features influencing the development and changes in their own and other locations.
- To investigate the influence of the physical terrain of a region and the availability of building space, on where people make their homes.
- Classroom activities and fieldwork exploring questions such as, 'What is it like to live in a wet climate?' and 'Why do people live on or near rivers?'
- How and why settlements evolve in a particular way.
- An ability to recognize patterns of settlement development in relation to availability of resources, economic activity and human needs.

SKILLS FOR GEOGRAPHY

- Undertake local fieldwork looking at living in areas liable to flood.
- Focus on the locality of the school and contrast findings with living conditions in Borneo.
- Look at weather conditions affecting how and where people live.
- Consider how site conditions influence the weather.
- Consider the physical features of a place that make it a desirable settlement, such as access to food and building materials.
- Think about how local features, such as rivers, influence human activity.
- Use appropriate geographical terms.
- Use a variety of secondary sources to find geographical information.

BACKGROUND NOTES

Sabah is a state of Malaysia in northern Borneo. It is bounded on the north by the South China Sea, on the north-east by the Sulu Sea, and on the south-east by the Celebes Sea. The south borders Kalamantan which is part of Indonesia. It is extremely mountainous and the only useful lowland is situated around its 1,400 kilometres of coastline. It has three navigable rivers:

Kinabatangan, Labuk and Padas. These are important for providing a main diet of fish and for moving wood produced by the forestry industry.

Fishing communities have lived along the rivers for hundreds of years. They are the Dayak people. The construction of their homes has remained the same for centuries because they continue to use the same building techniques and materials, such as the timber that is in abundance locally.

The climate here is tropical, with two monsoons per year. The wet season lasts from November to March and the dry season from June to October. Rainfall can reach 6,100 mm per year in the mountains. The foundations of the Dayak houses must be extremely strong to withstand this kind of rainfall and the pressure of the water flowing down the rivers to the sea.

The houses are constructed by driving sharpened tree trunks into the ground or the river-bed. In some areas, if resources are available, a hole is dug first during the dry season and concrete is poured in to give the stilts stronger foundations.

Many homes all over the world are constructed on stilts. Some are built to stand above the water, such as those in Ganvie, Dahomey, Africa. Others, such as those in Bangladesh, are on dry land for most of the year but are raised to avoid the floods of the monsoon. Stilts help keep these homes cool as well as providing shelter for animals.

Venice in Italy was built on marshland. The foundations were created by driving thousands of larch poles into the clay below. In the Netherlands, similar foundations were also needed. Today concrete piles are used instead of wooden stilts.

'When I was a little girl, I lived in what was then British Guiana (now Guyana), South America. Georgetown was below sea-level so the houses were built on stilts because of the risk from flooding. Being on stilts also kept the house cool along with the shutters on the windows. We used to play under the house. It was a really good place to play.'
D. WILTON, OXFORDSHIRE

DISCUSSION POINTS

1. Ask the children to describe the parts of their homes designed to cope with British rainfall, such as sloping roofs and guttering.

• Discuss children's experience of flooding. Was it first hand, or on television?

• How have people in Britain prepared for flooding? For example: the Thames Barrier.

• Consider the areas of Britain that are susceptible to flooding. Why are no houses built on stilts in these regions?

2. Discuss the design of stilt houses.

• Do the children think the stilts could support anything other than a wooden house?

• When the river is low, how would they climb from their boat up to the house?

CLASSROOM ACTIVITIES

SCIENCE KS1: POS 1A,B,C, 2A; EIS 1A, 3A,C.; K.S.2: POS 1A, B,C, 3A.; EIS 1A,B,C,D,E, 3C,E.
Buildings need foundations so they do not sink into the ground or blow over in strong winds. Examine how simple foundations work.
1. Fill a tray with damp sand.
2. Using a variety of coins, see how far you can press them down into the sand. Does their size make any difference?
3. Place the smallest coin on top of a larger, strong cardboard disc. Can you press them down as far as before?
4. Cut a piece of dowelling to match the depth of the sand. Put the coin over the dowelling. Can the coin sink? Discuss your understanding of how these foundations work.

D&T K.S.1: 1A,B, 2A,B, 3B,C,D,E,F, 4A,B,C,E,F, 5B,E; K.S.2: 1A,B, 2A,B, 3A,B,C,D,F,G, 4A,B,C,E,F,G, 5A,B,E.
Using twigs of similar size, design and make a model stilt house to withstand weather conditions outside. How far must you drive the stilts into the earth to keep the building stable? How does rain affect the foundations? Monitor the designs over a period of weeks.

SCIENCE K.S.1: POS 1A,B, 2A; EIS 1A,B,C, 2A,B, 3C,D,E,F; K.S.2: 1A,B, 2A, 4A; EIS 1A,B,D, 2B, 3B,C,D,E.
Test the suitability of a variety of materials, such as moss, clay and Plasticine, for blocking any holes in the roof of your model house to prevent rain getting in. What criteria will you use for assessment?

D&T K.S.1: 1A,B, 2A,B, 3A,B,C,D,E,F, 4A,B,C,E,F, 5B,E; K.S.2: 1A,B, 2A,B, 3A,B,C,D,F,G, 4A,B,C,E,F,G, 5A,B,E.
Ladders are used to enter houses on stilts. They are easy to make and can be pulled up if the water flows too quickly. Make a ladder suitable for climbing into a bunk bed, using rolled-up newspapers or other scrap materials. How can you safely test the strength of your ladder?

SCIENCE K.S.1: POS 1C, 2A, 3, 4A; LPLP 4A,B, 5A,B; K.S.2: 1C, 2A, 3B, 4A,C; LPLT 1A,B, 4A, 5A,C,D.
Many animals are adapted to living in and around water. Make a list and then a chart to show classifications, such as mollusc, insect, amphibian, reptile, fish, bird, mammal. Sort them into those that live mainly in the water, on the water, or at the water's edge. Find out which are carnivores (meat-eaters), omnivores (they eat meat and plants) or herbivores (they only eat plants). Devise a food chain for a watery environment. Make a Venn diagram to show which animals live in or around a pond, a river or the sea. Choose one animal to study in detail. Find out about its life cycle, any specially-adapted features, and its way of life.

FOLLOW-UP WORK

GEO K.S.2: 9B.
Find out where the main fishing industries of Britain are located. Where do the fishermen live? Are there any rivers that are particularly good for fishing?

GEO K.S.1: 2A, 3A.
Look for damp or wet places in your area where houses on stilts could be built. Design a modern house on stilts.

21

PHOTO

7

HOMES AROUND THE WORLD

HONG KONG HAS MANY TALL BUILDINGS

AREAS FOR STUDY

- An appreciation of the physical and human features influencing the development and changes in their own and other locations.
- To investigate the influence of the physical terrain of a region and the availability of building land on which people can erect their homes.
- Classroom activities and fieldwork exploring questions such as, 'What is it like to live in a crowded city?' and 'Why do people live cities?'
- How and why settlements evolve in a particular way.
- An ability to recognize patterns of settlement development in relation to availability of resources, economic activity and human needs.

SKILLS FOR GEOGRAPHY

- Undertake local fieldwork, looking at living in densely populated areas.
- Focus on locality of school and contrast findings with living conditions in Hong Kong.
- Observe and record similarities in city life throughout the world.
- Consider the influence of economic activity on the size and development of a settlement.
- Discover how land settlement can be used in a combination of ways, such as housing, transport and industry.
- Consider the physical features of a place that make it a desirable settlement, such as being a seaport, or availability of work.
- Think about how buildings can affect the quality of the environment, for example motorways.
- Use appropriate geographical terms.
- Use a variety of secondary sources to find geographical information.

BACKGROUND NOTES

Hong Kong comprises three main areas: Hong Kong Island and tiny surrounding islands; the mainland, bordered to the north by China; and the New Territories. Much of the land is hilly, most of the lowlands have been reclaimed from the sea. In total there are 1,076 square kilometres.

Hong Kong plays a significant role in the world economy. It is a major international finance centre with several stock exchanges. It has a large manufacturing industry that includes textiles and shipbuilding. Fishing and the export of fish is another major industry. Its large natural harbour has made it an important port for shipping from around the world.

Hong Kong has a sophisticated transport system. Kowloon houses a major international airport. There are also many kilometres of modern roads with a high vehicle density, a railway network, and ferries and hydrofoils linking the islands.

With an estimated population of five-and-a-half million (London has fewer than seven million people) and approximately 5,000 people per square kilometre, Hong Kong is short of building land. Most people have no alternative to high-rise living. It is estimated that the world population could increase to ten billion by the middle of the twenty-first century. Asia, including Hong Kong, will be central to this growth. Housing plans are already in preparation to cater for the extra people. In many places the only way is up.

The physical expansion of many cities is restricted by their geographical locations. There are natural barriers, such as the sea, mountains or desert. Unable to spread out as the population increases, the people have little choice but to build high-rise offices and homes. Examples of this are Manhattan in New York, which is built on an island, and Rio De Janeiro in Brazil, which is surrounded by high mountains.

DISCUSSION POINTS

1. Encourage discussion to help children to understand density of population.
- Is their school population large or small?
- Compare it to others, including secondary schools in the area.
- Discuss the number of people living in their locality. Is it densely populated?
- Discuss the differences between towns and villages, particularly relating to the availability or potential of jobs.

2. Why do most people in Hong Kong have to live near their work?
• Discuss the development in Britain of suburbs with enough space for building.
• How do people commute from the suburbs to their work?

3. Discuss with the children how the positions of their homes relate to other buildings and open space.
• How close are their neighbours?
• Do they have a garden?
• What sort of view is there from their home?
• Can they hang their washing outside?
• Why are there washing poles from the windows in the picture on the photocard?
• If there is no room for washing, where do the children play?
• Discuss the advantages and disadvantages of living in a crowded city.
• Britain is made up of a series of islands. Is it comparable to Hong Kong?

CLASSROOM ACTIVITIES

GEO K.S.1: 3A, 5A; K.S.2: 1B, 2A, 5B, 7A, 10A. Much of the lowland in Hong Kong has been reclaimed from the sea. This investigation may help you understand why that was necessary. In a plastic bowl or tank, make mountains using old Plasticine. Decide on the shapes you want for your mountains. Make sure they are joined together by 'land'. Now pour water half-way up the bowl. Describe what has happened. Which parts of the mountains are above water? Are there any flat areas where cities could be built? Are there any stretches of land available for travelling between the mountains?

MATHS K.S.1: UAM 1A, 3D, 5B; K.S.2: UAM 1A,B,C, 3B; HD 1A,B, 2B,D. Conduct a housing survey in your school. What kind of home do most people live in? Is this affected by the type of area in which they live, or the jobs they do? Record your results graphically.

ENG K.S.1: W 1A,B,C; K.S.2: W 1A,B,C. IT K.S.1: 1A, 2A,B,C; K.S.2: 1B,C, 2A,B,C. Devise a questionnaire that will encourage people in your school to give information about the advantages and disadvantages of their housing. Use a computer to collate and represent your findings.

MATHS K.S.1: UAM 1A, 2A; N 1A, 2A, 3C,D, 4A,B; K.S.2: UAM 1A,B, 2A,B,C, 3A; N 1A, 3C,D,E,F, 4A,B,C. A block of flats under construction is arranged with four flats on each floor. Twenty-four families need housing. How many storeys high does the block need to be? Make up similar problems for your friends to solve.

D&T K.S.1: 1A,B, 2A,B, 3A,B,C,D,E,F, 4A,B,C,E,F, 5A,B,D,E,F,G; K.S.2: 1A,B, 2A,B,C, 3A,B,C,D,F,G, 4A,B,C,E,F,G, 5A,C,E,G,H,I. Look at the picture on the photocard. How do the people get their washing in and out? Design and make a system that would avoid pulling the pole in and out. Is there information available in the photograph that may help you with your design?

FOLLOW-UP WORK

HIST K.S.1: KE 4A; K.S.2: KE 4A. Find out about the tallest buildings in your locality. What are they used for? What are they made from? Why were they built so high? Find out where the first skyscrapers were built. Where was the first skyscraper in Europe? What is the highest building in Britain?

RESOURCES FOR THE CLASSROOM

LOOK! HEAR! TALKING TOPICS
Software with simple work on the types of homes found in Britain. From Sherston Software Ltd, Angel House, Sherston, Malmesbury, Wiltshire SN16 0LH. Tel: 01666 840433.

HOMES
Available from PCET Wallcharts, 27 Kirshen Road, London W13 0UD. Tel: 0181 567 9206. Also *THE BUILT ENVIRONMENT* – a chart showing a range of houses.

23

PHOTO
8
HOMES AROUND THE WORLD

LIVING AND WORKING ON THE RIVER LI IN CHINA

AREAS FOR STUDY

- An appreciation of the physical and human features influencing the development and changes locally and in other places.
- To investigate the influence of the physical terrain of a region and the availability of building space on where people choose to make their homes.
- Classroom activities and fieldwork exploring questions such as, 'What is it like to live on a boat?' and 'Why do people live on the river?'
- How and why settlements evolve in a particular way.
- An ability to recognize patterns of settlement development in relation to availability of resources, economic activity and human needs.

SKILLS FOR GEOGRAPHY

- Undertake local fieldwork looking at living on houseboats.
- Contrast the locality of the school with living conditions in China.
- Look at weather conditions affecting how and where people live.
- Consider the physical features of a place that make it a desirable settlement.
- How the features of a locality, such as a river, influence human activity.
- Use appropriate geographical terms.
- Use a variety of secondary sources to find geographical information.

BACKGROUND NOTES

Sampans are river skiffs used for fishing, transporting freight and people, and as mobile shops and houseboats. They are traditional transport not only in China but throughout Asia. Usually flat-bottomed, they are propelled from the stern (the back of the boat) by a large sweep or by short oars at the sides. They are sometimes rigged with four-cornered, thick, cotton sails that are braced with strips of bamboo. Living accommodation and shelter for goods is usually a cabin covering part or all of the deck. It is constructed of matting or cloth with an arched or boxed support.

Houseboats are found on rivers, canals and in harbours. Originally they were trade-linked. Today, they are also an alternative means of housing in overcrowded cities such as Hong Kong, or Ho Chi Minh City in South Vietnam. Throughout history people have chosen to live on the water as a means of protection from enemies or flooding. The Romans used boats as palaces and temples. Barges are still a popular means of transportation of heavy goods in northern Europe, on the Rhine for example. These journeys are slow and the bargees live on board. In Britain many of the traditional canal narrowboats are no longer used for commercial transport. They have been converted to holiday craft or houseboats.

'I live on a narrowboat because it gives me peace, privacy and personal space. I am independent, self-contained and free to move at a moment's notice.'
MR COMPREY, NARROWBOAT OWNER

' I like it because it's a quick whoosh and that's all your housework done. It takes about thirty minutes and that's a good clean, then I can do the things I want to do like reading.'
EVE, NARROWBOAT OWNER

Many people have homes on board boats, such as the crews of large ships or submarines. These people are provided with many of the comforts they are accustomed to at home on dry land.

DISCUSSION POINTS

1. Discuss why most houseboats are found on rivers and in harbours rather than on the open sea. Try to incorporate the differences between river-sailing and sea–sailing, such as currents and tides.

2. What similarities can the children see between their own living accommodation and the facilities available on a sampan?
- What advantages can they see in this lifestyle?
- Discuss ways in which these Chinese people may cook their food. Draw on children's experiences of portable cookers, such as camping stoves.

- Discuss children's personal experiences of houseboats, barges and holiday boats.

3. The sampan in the picture on the photocard is a mobile shop as well as a house.
- What is it selling?
- What are the children's experiences of mobile shops? Why are they popular in certain places?

CLASSROOM ACTIVITIES

SCIENCE K.S.1: POS 1A,B,C, 2A, 3, 4A,B; EIS 1A,B,C, 2B,C, 3A,C,D,E,F; MP 1A,C, 2A; PP 2A,B,C; K.S.2: POS 1A,B,C, 2A,B, 3A,B, 4A,C; EIS 1A,B,C,D, 2B,C, 3A,B,C,D,E; MP 1A; PP 2B,G,H.

A sampan has a flat bottom. What are the advantages and disadvantages of this type of hull? Make a variety of boats from wood, paper, Plasticine, foil or any other suitable material. Which is the most successful shape? Devise a variety of tests to investigate the stability of your boats in water.

SCIENCE K.S.1: POS 1A,B, 2A,B, 3; EIS 1A,B, 2B,C, 3C,D,E; PP 1A,B,C; K.S.2: POS 1A,B, 2A,B, 3A,B, 4A; EIS 1A,B,C, 2B,C, 3B,C,D,E; PP 2B,C,F,G,H.

In a water tray, create currents and different sailing conditions. Contrast the tides and currents of a river or the sea, and the relative calm of a canal. How can you create the weather conditions that would affect the behaviour of the water?

MUSIC K.S.1: 2A,B,C,D,E,G, 4A,B,C,D,F, 5E,G; K.S.2: 2A,B,C,D,E,G, 4A,B,C,D,F, 5E,G.

Using a range of musical instruments, compose music of a suitable mood and tempo to reflect the water conditions you have created.

SCIENCE K.S.2: POS 1C, 2A,B,C, 3B, 4A; PP 2B,C, 4A,D. MATHS K.S.2: UAM 1A,B,C, 2A, 3A; SSM 4A; HD 2A.

Boats on estuaries and close to seashores are affected by the pull of the tides. Can you find out what causes tides? Using tide-tables, look up some tide times for a month and convert the figures into a graph. Make up some questions for a friend to answer using your graph, for example 'What time is low tide on Monday 7 March?'

SCIENCE K.S.1: POS 1A,B, 2A, 3, 4A; EIS 1A,B, 2B,C, 3A,D,E,F; MP 1A,E; 2A; PP 2B,C; K.S.2: POS 1A,B, 2A,B, 3A, 4A; EIS 1A,B,D, 2B,C, 3B,C,D,E; MP 1A; PP 2B,C,G. D&T K.S.1: 1A,B, 2A,B,C, 3A,B,C,D, E,F, 4A,B,C,E,F; K.S.2: 1A,B, 2A,B,C, 3A,B,C,D, E,F,G,

Find out how boats stop. Explore different methods. Make your own anchor. What would be the most effective way of mooring a sampan for the night? Consider that there may not be land-space available for mooring because of the number of boats.

SCIENCE K.S.1: POS 1A,B, 2A, 3, 4A,B; EIS 1A,B,C, 2B,C, 3A,B,C,D E,F; MP 1A,E; PP 2B,C,D; K.S.2: POS 1A,B, 2A,B, 3A,B, 4A,C; EIS 1A,B,D, 2B,C, 3B,C,D,E; MP 1A; PP 2B,C,F,G,H. MATHS K.S.1: UAM 1A, 2A 3A; N C; K.S.2: UAM 1A,B,C, 2A, 3A; N 2A,C.

Look at pictures of different types of sails. Consider their size, shape, what they are made of, and their rigging. Make a variety of sails and investigate sail power. How can you ensure you conduct fair tests? Which is the most effective shape? Can you calculate the surface area of your sails?

ART K.S.1: 1, 2B, 4D, 5C; 7A,B,C,D,E,F; 8A,C,D,E,F; K.S.2: 1, 2B, 4D, 5C, 7A,B,C,D,E,F, 8A,C,D,E,F. **D&T** K.S.1: 1A,B, 2A,B,C, 3A,B,C,D,E,F, 4A,B,C,E,F; K.S.2: 1A,B, 2A,B,C, 3A,B,C,D,E,F,G, 4A,B,C,E,F,G.

Sampans have very simple cabins. Can you reproduce something similar from material such as woven paper? Some houseboats contain every modern convenience. Design a luxury cabin for your houseboat.

FOLLOW-UP WORK

HISTORY K.S.1: POS 1B; KE 1A,B, 2C, 3A; K.S.2: KE 1A,B, 2C, 4A. **MUSIC** K.S.1: 1A,2B,C, 3A, 4A,B, 5A,C,D, 6C; K.S.2: 1A, 2B,C, 3A, 4A,B, 5A,C,D, 6C.

Investigate the development of boats over the years. Find out what life was like for sailors in the past. Many sailors used to sing sea shanties to help them keep a rhythm for their work. Collect as many shanties as you can for singing. Can any of these be sung as rounds?

ART K.S.1: 1, 2B, 4C,D, 7A,B, 8A,B,E; K.S.2: 1, 2B, 4C,D, 7A,B, 8A,B,E.

Visit a nearby river or canal and sketch the different shapes of the hulls of the boats. What is the function of each craft? In what ways does the function affect the design?

ART K.S.1: 1, 2B, 4B,C,D, 5B,C, 7A,B, 8A,B,D,E,F, 9A,B,C,D,E; K.S.2: 1, 2B, 4B,C,D, 5B,C, 7A,B, 8A,B,D,E,F, 9A,B,C,D,E.

Traditional British narrowboats are noted for the colourful designs painted on the outside. Collect pictures of decorated boats from around the world. Design your own patterns.

GEO K.S.1: 1B,C, 3A,E; K.S.2: 1B,D, 2A, 3D, 4, 5A, 6, 7A,B.

Mark the major rivers of Britain on a map. What are the major rivers in other countries? List them, marking which countries they go through. Can you find the six longest rivers in the world?

BOOKS FOR THE CLASSROOM

THE STORY OF PING
by Majorie Flack and Kurt Weise (Red Fox 1994)
An adventure story of Ping, a duckling who lives on a junk on the Yangtse River.

SNOWY
by Berlie Doherty (Harper Collins 1993)
Snowy the boat-horse pulls the narrowboat and gives horse rides, providing the income for Rachel's family.

STILL WATERS
by Pratima Mitchell (Red Fox 1994)
A novel about two children from different cultures who find a common bond; one lives on a houseboat and the other has done in the past. Their experiences become woven into a tale that explores a range of current issues.

BADGER ON THE BARGE
Janni Howker (Harper Collins 1994)
An adventure story centring around Badger, an older woman who lives on a barge.

NOAH'S ARK
by Jane Ray (Orchard 1995)
Perhaps the most famous of houseboats.

GO NOAH GO
by John Agard (Pic Knight 1992)
An ideal picture book for any classroom.

PLACES TO VISIT

THE BOAT MUSEUM, South Pier Road, Ellesmere Port, South Wirral L65 4FW.
Tel. 0151 355 5017.
Their collection includes a narrowboat. They can provide a visiting guide for schools which includes educational material.

USING THE ACTIVITY SHEET NO: 4

Instructions are given for folding a paper boat similar to a sampan. Children then have the choice of designing their own simple cabin, oars and sails for the sampan, and artefacts for sale.

MAKE A PAPER SAMPAN

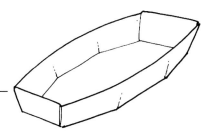

ACTIVITY SHEET 4

Name.. Class..

You will need:
  scissors, glue, coloured pencils.

1. Cut out the shape along
   the solid lines. _____

2. Fold the paper along the
   lines with dashes. - - - - - - - - -

3. Cut along the lines with
   dots and dashes. - · - · - · - · -

3. Fold the flaps C and D on
   to B and tuck the flaps E and
   F underneath the bottom of
   the boat.

4. Glue the flaps C and D on
   to B.

5. Fold down A on top of C
   and D and glue down.

6. Glue E and F to the bottom
   of the boat.

7. Using the scrap paper left
   over, design and make:
   • a cabin for the sampan
   • oars
   • a mast
   • sails
   • seats
   • things to sell

8. Decorate the outside and
   inside of your sampan so it
   looks as though it is made
   of wood.

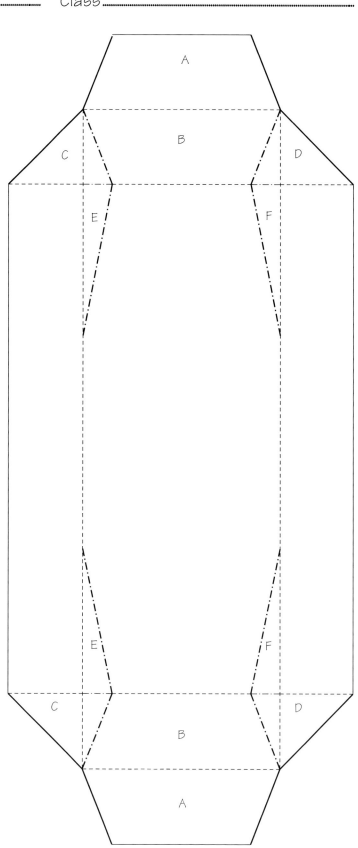

WAYLAND PUBLISHERS LTD, 61 WESTERN ROAD, HOVE, EAST SUSSEX BN3 1JD

HOMES AROUND THE WORLD

PHOTO

9

HOMES AROUND THE WORLD

CHALETS ARE HOUSES BUILT IN THE MOUNTAINS

AREAS OF STUDY

- An appreciation of the physical and human features influencing development and changes locally and in other places.
- To investigate the influence of climate on how people make their homes.
- Classroom activities and fieldwork exploring questions such as, 'What is it like to live in a cold climate?' and 'How do people survive?'
- How and why settlements evolve in a particular way.
- An ability to recognize patterns of settlement development in relation to availability of resources, economic activity and human needs.

SKILLS FOR GEOGRAPHY

- Undertake local fieldwork looking at surviving in cold weather.
- Focus on the locality of school and contrast findings with living conditions in the Alps.
- Look at weather conditions affecting how and where people live.
- Consider how site conditions influence the weather, extremes of weather and seasonal weather patterns.
- Consider the physical features of a place that make it a desirable settlement, such as grazing land and access to building materials.
- Think about how features of a locality, for example mountains, influence human activity.
- Use appropriate geographical terms.
- Use a variety of secondary sources to find geographical information.

BACKGROUND NOTES

Alpine chalets are still built in the traditional style with naturally-seasoned timber from local wood yards. Often the frames are made from hardwood and the outer panelling from softwood. Roofs are either wooden shingle, stone or slate. Their long, sloping style deters snow-slides and keeps the snow on the roof as an insulator. The broad eaves offer valuable storage space for neatly-stacked wood fuel. Although wooden houses are easy to heat, they also allow heat to escape through cracks in the floors, walls and roofs. Insulation is very

important. Modern chalets employ modern materials for insulation. Double- or triple- glazing traps air between the layers of glass and restricts heat loss through windows. Cavity walls have a gap between inner and outer walls which traps air or can be filled with special insulating materials. Insulation blocks are lightweight heat-retaining bricks coated on one side with insulating material. In the loft or attic, layers of insulating fibreglass or mineral wool are rolled out on to the floor. Carpets and rugs throughout the house prevent heat loss through the floors. Close-fitting doors and porches prevent heat escaping. Circulation of air inside buildings is important to prevent them from becoming damp.

Chalet-style houses, such as those in the Alps, are found in most mountainous regions, including Japan. Wherever possible they are built facing south to take full advantage of the sun.

DISCUSSION POINTS

1. Encourage children to share their own experiences of cold weather and snow.
- Do they enjoy it?
- How do they and their families prepare for cold weather, for example thicker clothing, anti-freeze for the car and extra heating in the house?
- Discuss the disadvantages of cold weather, such as burst pipes, and danger from icy roads and pavements.
- Discuss whether they think people living in Britain are as prepared for cold weather as those living in the Alps.

2. Discuss which months are more likely to have snow in Britain.
- What kind of weather conditions do the children think cause snow?
- Do all parts of Britain have the same amount of snow?

3. Ask the children to look closely at the photocard and describe the landscape.
- How can the landscape affect the weather?
- Can any children share their personal experiences of mountainous regions similar to the Alps?

CLASSROOM ACTIVITIES

GEO K.S.1: 1c, 3e, 5a; **K.S.2:** 1a,b,d, 2b,c, 3d.

Use a globe to locate the mountains of the world. Do children notice anything about their position? Use a map to find highlands in Britain.

SCIENCE K.S.1: POS 1a,b,c, 2a,b, 3, 4a,b; **EIS** 1a,b,c, 2a,b,c, 3a,c,d,e,f; **MP** 1a,b,c,e; **K.S.2: POS** 1a,b,c, 2a,b,c, 3a,b, 4a,b,c; **EIS** 1a,b,c,d, 2a,b,c, 3a,b,c,d,e; **MP** 1a,b.

Investigate the best materials for insulation.
1. Fill a bottle with hot water and put a cork in the top. Push a thermometer through the cork.
2. Wrap the bottle in an insulating material.
3. Record the temperature every 5 minutes for 20 minutes.
4. Repeat with other materials.
5. Record results on a bar chart.
6. Examine each material with a hand lens. Compare the structure with that of the least-effective insulating material.
7. Record your results.

SCIENCE K.S.1: POS 1a,b,c, 2a,b 3, 4a,b; **EIS** 1a,b,c, 2a,b,c, 3a,c,d,e,f; **MP** 1a,b,c,e; **K.S.2: POS** 1a,b,c, 2a,b,c, 3a,b, 4a,b,c; **EIS** 1a,b,c,d, 2a,b,c, 3a,b,c,d,e; **MP** 1a,b.

Which of these would be the best insulator: plastic, foil, bubblewrap, corrugated cardboard, or cotton wool? Put them in order and give reasons for your choice of position for each. Repeat the insulation investigation on these materials. Were you right? Were there any surprises? Record what happened.

SCIENCE K.S.1: POS 1a,b,c, 2a,b, 3, 4a,b; **EIS** 1a,b,c, 2a,b,c, 3a,c,d,e,f; **MP** 1a, 2b; **K.S.2: POS** 1a,b,c, 2a,b,c, 3a,b, 4a,b,c; **EIS** 1a,b,c, 2a,b,c, 3a,b,c,d,e; **MP** 1e, 2b.

Using measuring containers, such as medicine cups, carefully fill each to the first mark with liquids such as water, oil or white spirit. Place these on a tray in the freezer compartment of a refrigerator. Check them every 15 minutes. What happens to them? Record everything you notice. What do you think you could add to water to stop it freezing?

SCIENCE K.S.1: POS 1a,b,c, 2a,b, 3, 4a,b; **EIS** 1a,b,c, 2a,b,c, 3a,c,d,e,f; **MP** 1a,b,c,e; **K.S.2: POS** 1a,b,c, 2a,b,c, 3a,b, 4a,b,c; **EIS** 1a,b,c,d, 2a,b,c, 3a,b,c,d,e; **MP** 1a,b.

Make a collection of building materials, including brick, metal and wood. Devise tests to investigate their insulating properties. A quick method is to use your sense of touch: those that feel cold carry the heat away from your fingers and are conductors (poor insulators); those that feel warm to touch do not carry the heat away so quickly and are insulators.

GEO K.S.1: 1c, 3e, 5a; **K.S.2:** 1a,b,d, 2b,c, 3d.

Using information books, locate the mountain ranges of the world. Are they in hot and cold countries? Find the highest mountain.

GEO K.S.1: 1a, 2b, 5c,d; **K.S.2:** 1c, 2a, 5a, 8a,c.

Find out about other types of housing in mountainous regions. What do they have in common with an Alpine chalet?

SCIENCE K.S.1: POS 1b,c, 2a,b, 3, 4a, 5a,b; **EIS** 1a, 2a,c; **MP** 1a,b,c,d,e; **K.S.2: POS** 1b,c, 2a,b,c, 3a,b, 4a, 5a,b; **EIS** 1a, 2b, 3b,c,d,e; **MP** 1a,b.

Examine a range of insulating materials used in the home. You will need to wear gloves and face masks for this.

USING THE ACTIVITY SHEET NO: 5

A weather calendar is provided where children can draw their idea of the weather conditions for each month. Suggestions are made for symbols that could be used to represent the kinds of weather. Their weather calendars could be used as a starting point for discussing variability of weather conditions, seasonal norms and so on.

BOOKS FOR THE CLASSROOM

HEIDI
by Johanna Spyri
A classic children's novel set in Switzerland.

29

A CALENDAR OF THE WEATHER

ACTIVITY SHEET 5

Name .... Class ....

January	February	March	April	May	June
Is in the season of ____ winter	Is in the season of ____ winter	Is in the season of ____	Is in the season of ____	Is in the season of ____	Is in the season of ____
July	August	September	October	November	December
Is in the season of ____	Is in the season of ____	Is in the season of ____	Is in the season of ____	Is in the season of ____	Is in the season of ____

- ■ Fill in the name of the season that each month is in. For example, January is in winter.

- ■ Do you know what kind of weather to expect each month?

- ■ Draw a symbol or symbols in each box to show what you think the weather will be like.

- ■ You can also make up your own symbols, but remember to make a key.

- ■ Compare your calendar with those made by your friends. Have you got the same symbols?

- ■ Is the weather always the same each year?

temperature

sunshine

wind

rain

sun and clouds

snow

mist

frost and ice

WAYLAND PUBLISHERS LTD, 61 WESTERN ROAD, HOVE, EAST SUSSEX BN3 1JD

PHOTO
10

HOMES AROUND THE WORLD

A MALOCA IN THE RAINFOREST

AREAS OF STUDY:

- An appreciation of the physical and human features influencing the development and changes in their own and other locations.
- To investigate the influence of the physical terrain of a region and the availability of building space, on where people make their homes.
- Classroom activities and fieldwork exploring questions such as, 'What is it like to live in a wet climate?' and 'How do people survive living in a forest?'
- How and why settlements evolve in a particular way.
- An ability to recognize patterns of settlement development in relation to availability of resources, economic activity and human needs.

SKILLS FOR GEOGRAPHY

- Undertake local fieldwork looking at rainfall, and its effects on people's housing.
- Focus on the locality of your school and contrast findings of why and how people live communally in Britain with living conditions in a maloca, in Brazil.
- Look at the weather conditions affecting how and where people live.
- Consider extremes of weather conditions, such as rainfall.
- Consider the physical features of a place that make it a desirable settlement, such as access to food and building materials.
- Consider how the features of a locality, such as forest and river, influence human activity.
- Think about how and why people try to manage and sustain their environment.
- Think about how people can damage the environment and affect the people living there.
- Use appropriate geographical terms.
- Use a variety of secondary sources to find geographical information.

BACKGROUND NOTES

The Amazon Basin is a vast area containing one-fifth of the world's fresh water. It covers 6 million square kilometres. Much of its rainforest is located in Brazil and has been populated for thousands of years. The Portuguese settled there in 1500. They exploited the Indians, using them as slaves on their plantations. Many thousands of people died, and whole tribes were wiped out by European diseases, such as the common cold and smallpox, against which they had no resistance.

One of the largest surviving tribes is the Yanomi with an estimated population of 10,000. They live in harmony with the forest, taking what they need for survival and no more. Most live in extended family groups, in houses known as malocas which are also big enough to accommodate grandparents, aunts and uncles. Malocas vary in their style of architecture, and can house up to 150 people. They are single-storey dwellings of 30–40 metres across and can be circular, oval or rectangular. These communal homes are used for worship, eating, sleeping and meetings. Inside there may be separate areas for personal possessions, and places for hanging hammocks or laying sleeping mats. They are designed to withstand regular heavy rainfall (20,144 mm approximately each year) and are cool in hot weather and warm in cooler weather.

Sharing of tasks and co-operation is integral to Amazonian life but house building is strictly men's work. First the ground is cleared of vegetation and a plan marked out using vines. Timbers are cut from the forest using handmade axes. Posts and cross beams are lashed together with vines to create the main structure. Saplings are used where flexibility of shape is required and they, too, are attached with vines. Walls are filled in with broad palm leaves or bark panels. The roof is thatched with palm leaves or bundles of dried grass.

DISCUSSION POINTS

1. Discuss with the children what they notice about British weather.
- How would they describe it?

2. Ask them about their own homes and which parts are designed to provide protection from the rain, such as sloping roofs, guttering and drains, and also the types of materials used.

- What kinds of roofs can they describe in their locality? What are they made from?
- Have they ever seen a thatched roof? Where are these normally found?
- Discuss traditional building and availability of local materials.

3. Do any of the children have other relations, such as grandparents, living with them?
- What is the children's experience of communal living?
- Discuss their understanding of hostels, hotels, student housing and old people's homes.

4. What have the children heard about tropical rainforests. Share their knowledge and discuss the delicate balance of the ecosystem and how exploitation of land not only affects the lives of the inhabitants but also their own lives.

CLASSROOM ACTIVITIES

D&T KS1: 1A,B,C, 2A,B,C, 3A,B,C,D,E,F. 5B,C,D; **K.S.2:** 1A,B,C, 2A,B,C, 3A,B,C,D,E,F,G, 4A,B,C,D,E,F,G, 5A,E,F,H.	How do gutters and drainpipes work on a house? Simulate their design using construction straws. What do you need to do to ensure the water drains away?
SCIENCE K.S.1: MP 2B; **K.S.2:** MP 2B,C,D,E.	Allow the children to watch from a safe distance while an adult boils a kettle of water, and then condenses the water in a frying pan. Discuss the changes in state of water from liquid to water vapour and back to liquid again.
SCIENCE K.S.1: LPLT 3B, 4B, 5A,B; **K.S.2:** 3A, 4A, 5A,B.	Collect fresh leaves and examine their shape and the patterns of their veins. When it rains, how does the water drain off them? Using a dropper, simulate raindrops falling on leaves. Make careful notes of your observations. Why are palm leaves a popular choice for roofing in the rainforests?

D&T K.S.1: A,B,C, 2A,B,C, 4A,B,C,D,E,F, 5B,D,E; **K.S.2:** 1A,B,C, 2A,B,C, 4A,B,C,D,E,F,G, 5A,E,G,H,I.	Make a Lego house, and add beams to support the roof. Using leaves or straw, devise a method of thatching the roof so it is watertight. How will you attach the thatch so that it will not slip or blow off?
SCIENCE K.S.1: POS 1A,B, 2A,B,C, 3A, 4A,B, 5A,B; EIS 1A,B,C, 2A,B,C, 3A,B,C, D,F; LPLT 3B, 4B, 5A,B; MP 1D,E, 2A; **K.S.2:** POS 1A,B, 2A,B,C, 3A, 4A,C, 5A,B; EIS 1A,B,C,D,E, 2A,B,C, 3B,C,D,E; LPLT 3A,4A,5A,B; MP 1A.	Investigate how trees protect themselves from rain damage. Consider the shape of the tree and its leaves, the bark and their natural, water-resistant oils and structure. Record your findings with annotated diagrams. We use paint and varnish to prevent rain and damp from rotting wooden buildings. Following safety procedures, paint pieces of planed wood with prepared solutions and leave them to dry. Weigh and record the weight of each piece. Immerse in water overnight. The next day weigh them again. Record your observations and any conclusions you make. Did you follow the manufacturers' instructions? Can you prepare any natural solutions that you think would make wood waterproof. Repeat the experiment to test the success of your solutions.

FOLLOW-UP WORK

ENG K.S.1: R 1A,B,C, **W** 1A,B,C, 2B; **K.S.2: R** 1A,B,C, 2B,C; **W** 1A,B,C, 2A,B.	Research the environmental issues relating to the tropical rainforests of the Amazon Basin. Mount a campaign with posters and leaflets to raise people's awareness of the issues.
ENG R 1A,B,C; **K.S.2: R** 1A,B,C, 2B,C. **GEO K.S.2:** 8A,C; **SCIENCE K.S.2: MP** 2E.	What makes it rain? Use information books to investigate the rain cycle and illustrate your understanding of this with annotated diagrams.

11 CAIRO IS A HOT, DRY CITY IN EGYPT

AREAS OF STUDY:

- An appreciation of the physical and human features influencing the development and changes in their own and other locations.
- To investigate the influence of the physical terrain of a region and the availability of building space, on where people make their homes.
- Classroom activities and fieldwork exploring questions such as, 'What is it like to live in a hot, dry climate?' and 'What is it like to live in a crowded city?
- How and why settlements evolve in a particular way.
- An ability to recognize patterns of settlement development in relation to availability of resources, economic activity and human needs.

SKILLS FOR GEOGRAPHY

- Undertake local fieldwork, looking at keeping cool.
- Focus on the locality of your school to contrast how people cope with hot weather in Britain with methods used in Cairo.
- Look at the weather conditions affecting how and where people live.
- Consider how site conditions influence the weather.
- Observe and record similarities in city life throughout the world.
- Consider the physical features of a place that make it a desirable settlement, such as access to food and building materials.
- Look at how the features of the locality, for example being a seaport on the River Nile, influence human activity.
- Use appropriate geographical terms.
- Use a variety of secondary sources to find geographical information.

BACKGROUND NOTES

Cairo is a port, situated on the east bank of the River Nile. It is the capital of Egypt and the largest city of Africa and the Middle East. For over 1,000 years it has been the cultural centre of Islam. It has a modern business centre, large manufacturing industries and a successful tourist industry. There is a population of six million, and in the poorest areas of the city, there are estimated to be 100,000 people for each square kilometre. Around 90 per cent of Egypt is desert, and the climate consists of a hot season from May to September and a cool season from November to March. Extremes of temperature are experienced in both periods. Cairo can expect a meagre 28 mm of rain per year.

By the fourteenth century, Cairo was a large city with a population of 500,000, which was later considerably reduced by wars and the Black Death. Invaders contributed their own customs and styles of building. The French only occupied Cairo for three years and destroyed many old buildings to create wide avenues which still remain today. The British developed a modern urban centre during their lengthy occupation. After the First World War, rural Egyptians flocked to the city in search of work These people desperately needed housing, and homes were built in the traditional style, using local materials and age-old building techniques.

In hot, dry climates people are not only influenced by cost and availability of resources, but are also concerned with protecting themselves from the heat of the sun. In such climates, wood is scarce but mud is plentiful. Thick adobe walls keep out the intense heat of the sun in summer, and insulate the homes in winter. Limiting the number of windows and keeping them small restricts the heat but allows breezes to blow through. The houses are often crowded together along narrow streets so they shade each other from the heat of the sun. They are often whitewashed to deflect the radiation. Pitched roofs are unnecessary in dry climates. Flat roofs are quicker and easier to build, as well as creating outdoor rooms for cooler sleeping quarters or storage areas.

DISCUSSION POINTS

1. Discuss where the children have seen flat roofs in Britain, for example on extensions or on temporary classrooms.
• Discuss why children think most houses in Britain have pitched roofs.

33

2. What are the children's ideas for keeping the interior of a house cool?
• Contrast efforts for keeping cool with attempts in their own homes to insulate with curtains and fitted carpets.

3. Ask children to comment on all the different styles of housing there may be in their locality.
• Many of the houses in the picture on the photocard are very similar. What reasons can the children suggest for housing styles remaining the same?

CLASSROOM ACTIVITIES

SCIENCE K.S.1: POS 1A,B,C, 2A,B, 3, 4A,B; **EIS** 1A,B,C, 2A,B,C, 3A,B,C,D,E,F; **PP** 3A; **K.S.2: POS** 1A,B,C, 2A,B,C, 3A,B, 4A,B,C; **EIS** 1A,B,C,D, 2A,B,C, 3A,B,C,D,E; **MP** 1B; **PP** 1A,B,C.

Discuss which colours absorb heat and which deflect it. On the sunniest wall of your classroom, stick up different coloured sheets of paper. Let the sun shine on them for some time. Then feel each one to see which is the hottest. Record your results. Does everyone agree that this is a fair test? Can you devise another investigation to find out which colours absorb the heat and which reflect it?

ART K.S.1: 1, 2A, 3, 4B, 5B,C, 7,A,C,D,E,F, 8D,E,F, 9B,C,D,E; **K.S.2:** 1, 2A, 3, 4B, 5B,C, 7,A,C,D,E,F, 8D,E,F, 9B,C,D,E.

Colours are often described as warm and cold. Using patterns, create colour interpretations of hot and cold temperatures. Does everyone use similar colours? Look at the work of famous artists. How do they create climates and atmospheres using colour?

D&T K.S.1: 1A,B, 2A,B,C, 3A,B,C,D,E,F, 4A,B,C,E,F; **K.S.2:** 1A,B, 2A,B,C, 3A,B,C,D,E,F,G, 4A,B,C,E,F,G.

In hot countries, people often sleep on the roofs where they will catch the cool evening breezes. They need comfortable beds to sleep on and protection from insects, such as mosquitoes. Considering their needs, design and make a model bed that would keep them cool and offer protection. Think about your choice of materials. Which are cool and which act as insulators?

SCIENCE K.S.1: POS 1A,B,C, 2A,B, 3, 4A,B; **EIS** 1A,B,C, 2A,B,C, 3A,B,C,D,E,F; **MP** 1A,E; **K.S.2: POS** 1A,B,C, 2A,B,C, 3A,B, 4A,B,C; **EIS** 1A,B,C,D, 2A,B,C, 3A,B,C,D,E.

Make adobe bricks by digging clay from the school garden and mixing it with straw. How can you ensure the bricks are all the same size? Leave them to dry in the sunshine. How long does it take? How have they changed? What are the disadvantages of handmade bricks? How high can you build with them using mud as a mortar?

FOLLOW-UP WORK

ART K.S.1: 1, 2B, 3, 4C, 7A,C,D,F, 8A,D,F; **K.S.2:** 1, 2B, 3, 4C, 7A,C,D,F, 8A,D,F.

Divide a sheet of paper in half. On one half draw all the different ways you keep cool in very hot weather. Think about the clothes you wear, how you keep the house cool, the types of activities you do, the food you eat and the fluids you drink. On the other half, contrast these with how you keep warm.

Visit a travel agent and collect brochures of places in hot, dry climates. Cut out pictures of housing. How do they compare with those in Cairo?

PLACES TO VISIT

MUSEUM OF MANKIND, 6 Burlington Gardens, London W1X 2EX.
Tel : 0171 437 2224.

COMMONWEALTH INSTITUTE, Kensington High Street, London W8 6NQ.

THE MUSEUM OF WELSH LIFE, St Fagans, Cardiff CF5 6XB. Tel: 0122 569 441.

THE AVONCROFT MUSEUM OF HISTORIC BUILDINGS, Stoke Heath, Bromsgrove, Worcestershire B60 4JR. Tel: 015 278 31363. Displays include a fourteenth-century barn, a fifteenth-century merchant's house and a windmill.

PHOTO
12
HOMES AROUND THE WORLD

A SHANTY TOWN IN BOMBAY, INDIA

AREAS OF STUDY

- An appreciation of the physical and human features influencing the development and changes in their own and other locations.
- Investigate the influence of employment and wealth and the availability of building space, on where people make their homes.
- Classroom activities and fieldwork exploring questions such as, 'Why are some people unemployed?', 'Why are some people homeless?' 'What is it like to live in a crowded city?', and 'Why do people live in cities?'
- How and why settlements evolve in a particular way.
- An ability to recognize patterns of settlement development in relation to availability of resources, economic activity and human needs.

SKILLS FOR GEOGRAPHY

- Undertake local fieldwork looking at living in areas liable to flood.
- Focus on the locality of your school to explore evidence of homelessness and compare to conditions in Bombay.
- Appreciate the differences between settlements and that their location is affected by economic activity.
- Look at weather conditions affecting how and where people live.
- Observe and record similarities in city life throughout the world.
- Use appropriate geographical terms.
- Use a variety of secondary sources to find geographical information.

BACKGROUND NOTES

Situated in western India, Bombay developed around one of the world's largest natural harbours on the Arabian Sea. It was named Bom Bahia (Beautiful Bay) by the Portuguese in 1534. Steadily increasing in numbers, the population now stands at approximately 12·5 million. Bombay is India's leading financial centre, with extensive commercial and manufacturing industries. These include film-making, textile printing, publishing, shipbuilding, cotton, metal and chemical industries. The industrial areas extend to the north of the city, and beyond lie the suburbs and shanty towns. Most of the shanties have neither running water nor electricity. They provide a sharp contrast with the suburbs.

Homelessness occurs all over the world and is becoming a significant social problem for many cities. In 1994, over 120,000 households in England were recognized by local councils as homeless. Local authorities are obliged to provide accommodation for those declared 'not intentionally' homeless. With too few council houses available, many live in temporary accommodation such as bed–and–breakfast hotels. Other people are classed as 'intentionally' homeless, for example alcoholics or drug addicts, and the local authority has no obligation to provide permanent housing for them. These people sleep rough on the streets in doorways and cardboard boxes, in squats, or use emergency night shelters. Homeless young people over the age of seventeen, without children or disabilities, are not regarded as a priority by local authorities.

'I left because of problems at home. I don't like to go to the shelters because some of the people there can be violent or taking drugs. I often go round to various friends and spend one or two nights at their homes. I sell the Big Issue to earn some money.'
HOMELESS GIRL, LONDON

Locally, nationally and globally, voluntary organizations and some governments are working towards protecting those whose housing is threatened, and providing food and temporary shelter for the homeless. Overall the problems will continue until it is possible to provide adequate housing for people unable to pay for their own.

DISCUSSION POINTS

1. Have any of the children moved to a home in a different area? Perhaps some children have just moved to your school.
- How did they feel about leaving their friends?
- Can they describe packing up all their things?
- Did they have to leave anything behind?

2. Have any of the children seen refugees on the news or homeless people on the streets?
• Why do they think they are homeless?
• What do they notice about them?
• How do they think they keep warm and dry?

3. 'Home is where you make it.' Do children living in shanty towns enjoy life? What makes them happy? What experiences do your children share with shanty town children?
• Often shanty houses of two or three rooms can be home for maybe ten brothers and sisters. Do any of the children share a room – what problems sometimes occur? Do other children share the same problems?
• Do the children know of any scrapyards or places where they could find materials to build a temporary shelter?
• Where do they think the people in this shanty town may have found their building materials?

CLASSROOM ACTIVITIES

D&T K.S.1: 1A,B, 2A,B, 3B,C,D,E, 4A,B,C,E; K.S.2: 1A,B, 2A,B, 3B,C,D,E,F, 4A,B,C. Make a house out of scrap materials. Ensure it has windows, a door and a roof. Can you provide furnishing for it?

SCIENCE K.S.1: POS 1A,B, 2A,B, 3A, 4A; EIS 1A,B, 2A,B, 3A,C,D,E,F; MP 1A,B,D,E; K.S.2: POS 1A,B, 2A,B,C, 3A, 4C; EIS 1A,B,C, 3B,C,E; MP 1A,B. Find a cardboard box that is big enough for you to sit inside. Using scrap material, how can you insulate the box and protect it from wet? Record what you did in drawings and writing. How did the way you tackled this problem compare with others in the class?

ENGLISH K.S.1: W 1B,C; K.S.2: W 1A,B,C. Make up an acrostic (such as homeless) to illustrate the problems uncovered through the discussion.

ENGLISH K.S.1: SL 1A,B,D; K.S.2: SL 1A,C,D. Work with a partner to improvise short scenes about homelessness, for example packing possessions to flee the country on foot.

FOLLOW-UP WORK

ENGLISH K.S.1: W 1A,B,C, 2A,C,E; K.S.2: W 1A,B,C 2A,B,C,E. Write to Shelter, Oxfam or Save the Children for information about their work with homeless people.

BOOKS IN THE CLASSROOM

THE BED & BREAKFAST STAR
by Jacqueline Wilson (Transworld 1995)
Life in cramped bed-and-breakfast accommodation as seen through the eyes of a nine-year-old.

STREET CHILD
by Berlie Doherty (Collins 1995)
The life story of Jim Jarvis, the boy who inspired Dr Barnardo.

SHAKER LANE
by Alice and Martin Provensen (Walker 1991)
The eviction of a poor community to make way for the building of a dam.

PAST AND PRESENT: HOMELESSNESS
by Carole Seymour-Jones (Heinemann 1993)

COUNTRY TOPICS: INDIA
by Anita Ganeri and Rachel Wright (Watts 1994)

FOCUS ON INDIA
by Shahrukh A Husain (Evans Brothers 1991)

RESOURCES FOR THE CLASSROOM

SHELTER HOUSING AID, 88 Old Street, London EC1V 9HU.

OXFAM, 274, Banbury Road, Oxford OX2 7DZ. Tel: 01865 311311.

USING THE ACTIVITY SHEET NO: 6

Based on the information contained in the photocards, children are asked to locate certain houses on a world map.

A WORLD MAP

ACTIVITY SHEET 6

Name... Class...

Britain	China
Canada	Egypt
India	Borneo

■ Fill in the missing country.

1. Inuit house in ....

2. Stilt house in ....

3. Sampan in ....

4. Flat-roofed house in ....

5. Shanty town in ....

6. No. 10 Downing Street in ....

■ Draw arrows to pin-point the countries on the map. Use an atlas to help you.

WAYLAND PUBLISHERS LTD, 61 WESTERN ROAD, HOVE, EAST SUSSEX BN3 1JD

PHOTO **13** HOMES AROUND THE WORLD

BEDOUIN HERDSPEOPLE LIVE IN TENTS

AREAS OF STUDY

- An appreciation of the physical and human features influencing the development and changes in their own and other locations.
- To investigate the influence of the main employment of the population and the physical terrain of a region, on where people make their homes.
- Classroom activities and fieldwork exploring questions such as, 'What is it like to live in an arid climate?', and 'Why do people lead nomadic lifestyles?'
- An ability to recognize patterns of settlement development in relation to availability of resources, economic activity and human needs.

SKILLS FOR GEOGRAPHY

- Undertake local fieldwork looking at people who lead a nomadic life in the Britain.
- Focus on the locality of school and contrast findings with living conditions in the desert.
- Look at weather conditions affecting how and where people live.
- Consider the extremes of weather found in a desert climate.
- Consider how site conditions influence the weather.
- Think about how features of a locality influence human activity.
- Use appropriate geographical terms.
- Use a variety of secondary sources to find geographical information.

BACKGROUND NOTES

The Bedouin are nomadic Arabs who travel with their animals through the deserts of the Middle East and north Africa. Many Bedouin families have been forced to settle because over-grazing and water shortages have destroyed much of the grazing land. Only 5–10 per cent of the population now lead a full nomadic existence, and those that do farm sheep as well as goats and camels. The heat in the desert is terrific with daytime temperatures reaching 45 °C, but in winter months after sunset, the temperature can drop as low as 0 °C. Bedouin families live in tents

that can be adjusted to the temperature. They are made from strips of fabric, woven by the women from camel and goat hair and sometimes vegetable fibre. The cloth is dyed a dark colour, often black, perhaps so that the thick fabric will retain the heat of the sun to disperse in the cold evenings. The sides are draped with blankets that can be drawn back in hot weather. Women and children sleep at one side of the tent divided from the men by a curtain. The tents are normally erected by the women and consist of a frame comprising nine wooden poles secured by guy ropes which are attached to stakes hammered into the sand.

Nomadic people live all over the world, some in the harshest of territories. Many of Britain's travellers are descendants of Romanies who spread from India 1,000 years ago. They earn a living selling their handicrafts or from seasonal work, such as fruit-picking. Other travellers in Britain are show and fairground people. All travellers have their own style of mobile home which for many is still a tent or caravan. Wherever they roam, their traditional lifestyles are threatened by authorities who want them to conform, or restrictions either political, financial or climatic which affect the land they need for grazing, hunting and camping.

'We usually spend about a week in any one place. It's a hard life because you have to set up or pack up everytime. We go to sites where there is water which we pay for – it's usually on a meter. We pay our rates and things so we get pensions when we retire. My father and grandfather were both showmen, so you learn how to do things as you grow up. You learn to do lots of jobs. My young nephew is now really good at painting and welding and will also take a look at the engine if the lorry breaks down. We travel for about seven months of the year and then stay on a site in Norwich for a couple of months.'
FAIRGROUND SHOWMAN, EAST ANGLIA

DISCUSSION POINTS

1. Ask the children to think about the types of jobs that require people to travel, such as ice cream vendors in vans, circus and fairground workers, and door-to-door salespersons.
- Can the children describe their work?

2. Discuss the children's experience of temporary homes, such as caravans, tents and campervans.
• How does the lack of space and the need to carry their possessions affect them?
• How do the children know where they live?
• What landmarks help them find their homes?
• Can they suggest how Bedouins might locate their tents in a featureless landscape?

3. Discuss how British farmers look after herds of cows, sheep or goats.
• How do farming methods compare with those of the Bedouin?
• Why do shepherds in Britain rarely travel very far to find new grazing land?

CLASSROOM ACTIVITIES

ENGLISH K.S.1: W 1A,B,C; **K.S.2: W** 1A,B,C.
Imagine you are going camping. In your rucksack you have a tent and a sleeping bag. What other necessary items can you fit in? Make a list of what you need. You must also eat, drink and keep yourself clean.

D&T K.S.1: 1A, 5B,C,D,E,F,G; K.S.2: 1A, 5B,C,D, E,F,G. ENG K.S.1: W 1A,B,C; **K.S.2: W** 1A,B,C.
Erect a tent. How is it made? What materials are used? Would it stand up to windy weather, and keep you warm and dry? Does shape make a difference? How is it secured to the ground? Write about your tent comparing it to other designs. Use catalogues to help you describe specific parts and features.

ART K.S.1&2: 1A, 2C, 4D, 5C, 7A,B, C,D,E,F, 8A,B,C,D, E,F, 9B,C,D,E. D&T K.S.1&2: 1A,B, 2A,B, 3 A,B, C,D,E,F, 4A,B,C,E,F..
From the information you have gathered, design and make a prototype for your own tent using fabric. Consider how you will sew it together, make the needle holes watertight, and how you will secure it to the ground.

D&T: K.S.1: 1B, 3A, 4C,F; K.S.2: 1B, 3A, 4C,F.
How could Bedouins fasten their tents against sandstorms or the cold night air? Examine fasteners used for joining fabric. Can you devise some of your own methods?

ART K.S.1: 1A, 2C, 4D, 5C, 7A,B, C,D,E,F, 8A,B,C,D, E,F, 9B,C,D,E; K.S.2: 1A, 2C, 4D 5C, 7A,B,C,D,E,F, 8A,B,C,D,E,F, 9B,C, D,E. D&T K.S.1: 1A,B, 2A,B, 3A,B, C,D,E,F, 4A,B,C, E,F; K.S.2: 1A,B, 2A,B, 3A,B,C,D,F,G, 4A,B,C,E,F.
Look at some hand-woven fabric to find out how the patterns are made. Design a simple pattern on paper and reproduce it on a loom. Make a simple loom using two branches. Cut strings of equal length and tie them at both ends to the branches to form the warp. Hang the loom up and weight down the bottom end. Then weave the weft using a variety of materials such as sheep's wool, straw, strips of paper or coloured cloth to create the pattern you designed.

FOLLOW-UP WORK

ENGLISH K.S.1: SL 1C, 2B; **W** 1 A,B,C; **K.S.2: S.L.** 1C, 2B; **W** 1A,B,C.
What are the advantages of a nomadic lifestyle? Make a list of your views. Invite a traveller or backpacker into school. How does the reality compare with your ideas.

BOOKS FOR THE CLASSROOM

LEILA
by Sue Alexander (Hamish Hamilton 1988)
The story of a Bedouin girl whose brother goes in search of new pastures, never to return.

FIRESIDE TALES
by Duncan Williamson (Silkies 1993)
Traveller stories that have been handed down from generation to generation.

MOVING
by Michael Rosen (Puffin 1995)

HARRY MOVES HOUSE
by Chris Powling (Harper Collins 1993)

FAIRGROUND FAMILY
by Mog Johnson (A & C Black 1985)
One of many books in the Beans Series, which describes places, jobs or ways of life in many places of the world.

THE HOME OF THE BRITISH PRIME MINISTER

AREAS OF STUDY

- To investigate the influence of employment on where people make their homes.
- An ability to recognize patterns of settlement development in relation to availability of resources, economic activity and human needs.

SKILLS FOR GEOGRAPHY

- Undertake local fieldwork to investigate houses that were or are still related to the job of the occupant.
- Think about how features of the locality influence human activity.
- Use appropriate geographical terms.
- Use a variety of secondary sources to find geographical information.

BACKGROUND INFORMATION

Premiers all over the world live in official residences from which they work, or which are close to other official buildings from where they govern their countries. These homes have good communication systems, offices and rooms for meetings, and they are well-protected by strict security. Number 10 Downing Street is the official residence of the British prime minister. The plain brick houses of Downing Street were built in 1680 by Sir George Downing, a Member of Parliament. Number 10 became an official residence in 1732 when George II offered it to Sir Robert Walpole. Walpole would not accept the house for himself but accepted it as a home for future British prime ministers. Many subsequent prime ministers, who already had large homes, let the house to relatives and junior ministers. Number 11 Downing Street became the home for the chancellor of the exchequer in 1805. Many of the various British royal palaces are reserved for official duties and functions. The royal family lives in private apartments within the buildings.

Before the First World War, wealthy people employed a considerable number of servants to keep their large homes in order. The hours were long and arduous and most servants lived on the premises. They were poorly paid and had few opportunities for visiting friends and relatives. Domestic service was often the only option for women who needed to earn a living and provide a roof over their heads. Today some homes have live-in domestic staff and nannies, but modern transport allows many domestic workers to travel from their own homes.

A number of employers provide accommodation for employees who must be available for much of the time, or have sporadic and unusual hours. Some examples are vicars living in vicarages owned by the Church, tenant farmers who manage the land for the owner, publicans running brewery-owned public houses, and schoolkeepers with houses on the school site. On retirement these people must usually find another home.

'The problem with living in tied accommodation is that you are always on call, always at work. But being on-site means I have no travelling to do to get to work and the accommodation is free. When schoolkeepers retire, then our Union has arranged that the Local Council must offer us a choice of two alternative accommodations or else we could buy a place of our own.'
MR G. BRADSHAW, SCHOOLKEEPER, LONDON BOROUGH OF GREENWICH

People often use their own homes as a base for their business. Shopkeepers, weavers, millers, blacksmiths, bakers, cutlers, writers and craftspeople are examples. In the past places of work included living quarters for their own family and for any apprentices employed. In addition, many women with children took in sewing, laundry or piecemeal factory work. Today shopkeepers may live above or at the back of shops; some doctors and dentists may have surgeries in their homes; and owner-farmers usually have houses situated on their farmland.

With the advance of modern telecommunications systems, many new opportunities are arising for people to conduct a wide range of businesses from home, or to work at home connected electronically to the company that employs them. These developments are of particular benefit to mothers with small children.

DISCUSSION POINTS

1. Does your school have a schoolkeeper? Does this person live on the school premises?
• Do any other people in the locality have houses that go with their jobs?
• Discuss the signs that show people work from home, such as the plaques used by doctors.

2. Ask the children if any of them have visited stately homes or castles, such as those run by the National Trust or English Heritage.
• Find out if they were able to see any of the servants' quarters or working areas.
• Discuss how their conditions for working and living differed from the family who lived there.

3. Talk about local houses of special interest, or houses once owned by people with servants.
• Are these houses still homes for families?
• If, not, why do they think they have changed?
• In what ways have they changed?
• What are they used for now?

4. Ask the children to think of jobs that can be conducted from home.
• Do they know of anyone who works from home, such as a registered child-minder?

5. Find out if any of the children have any older brothers and sisters or other relatives who go away to college or university.
• How do they feel about them being away for long periods of time?
• What do their brothers or sisters think about being away from home?

6. Ask the children what they know about famous houses that feature in the news, such as Buckingham Palace.

CLASSROOM ACTIVITIES

HIST K.S.1:
POS 2; K.S.2:
KE 1A, 4B, 5A,B.
List in chronological order all the prime ministers that have been in office since Robert Walpole. Who was the monarch at the time of each? How many prime ministers have there been this century?

GEO K.S.2: 3D. Find out where the leaders of other countries live. Mark their homes on a map. What do you notice about their locations?

ART K.S.1: 1,
2A,C, 3, 4, 8D,E,F;
K.S.2: 1, 2A,C, 3,
4, 8D,E,F. ENG
K.S.1&2: W
1A,B,C.
Draw an imaginary house that you think would go with the job of a motor mechanic or a computer technician. Label specific design features to make your intentions clear.

ENG K.S.1&2 W
1A,B,C.
Describe how you imagine the inside of 10 Downing Street. Will it be an ordinary terraced house?

FOLLOW-UP WORK

ENG K.S.1: SL
1C, 2B; K.S.2: SL
1B,C. 2A,B.
Arrange to interview a vicar, a schoolkeeper, or a local artist. Ask them about the disadvantages and advantages of working from home.

HIST K.S.1:
POS: 2, KE 4A;
K.S.2: KE 4A.
Find out if any famous writers, poets or artists have lived and worked from a house in your area.

BOOKS FOR THE CLASSROOM

INSIDE A VICTORIAN HOUSE
edited by Jo Fletcher-Watson (The National Trust 1993)
This book, useful for all ages, describes everyday life on a large country estate.

A LIKELY LAD
by Gillian Avery (Red Fox 1992)
The story of a shop in Edwardian times.

THE APPRENTICE
by Leon Garfield (Puffin 1982)
A novel for more experienced readers about the life of Victorian apprentices.

A STRONG AND WILLING GIRL
by Dorothy Edwards (Mammoth 1994)
A short novel about a young maidservant's life at the beginning of Queen Victoria's reign. Suitable for reading aloud to younger children.

PHOTO
15

LOBI CHILDREN DECORATE THEIR HOMES

AREAS OF STUDY

- Classroom activities and fieldwork exploring questions such as, 'What is it like to live in a hot climate?' and 'Why do people decorate their homes?'
- How and why settlements evolve in a particular way.
- An ability to recognize patterns of settlement development in relation to availability of resources and human needs.

SKILLS FOR GEOGRAPHY

- Undertake local fieldwork looking at how people personalize their environment.
- Focus on the locality of school and contrast findings with living conditions in Ghana.
- Look at weather conditions affecting how and where people live.
- Consider the physical features of a place that make it a desirable settlement, for example access to building materials.
- Use appropriate geographical terms.
- Use a variety of secondary sources to find geographical information.

BACKGROUND INFORMATION

The Lobi people live in Ghana, where the climate is tropical with up to five months of torrential rain. They have a traditional lifestyle which is as yet not influenced by modern Africa. Originally a nomadic people, today they are mainly farmers. Building resources and tools are very few and settlements are sited close to a plentiful supply of clay which is used for building. The Lobi dwelling on the photocard houses an extended family of fifteen people.

Lobi houses are built by hand. A low wall approximately fifty centimetres high is modelled from clay and then left to dry. Consecutive walls are added until the required height and width is reached. Because of the heavy rains, the edges of the walls are sealed with cow dung, and the walls are painted with a solution made from plant sap to protect them from erosion. The overall appearance of each dwelling, known as a soukala, is rather

like a fortress. Safeguarding the family is of paramount importance. The lack of windows is a traditional feature, protecting the inhabitants from attack. The inside of each house is also completely modelled in clay, with ledges for sitting, sleeping and storage, granaries and ovens. The only light comes from the fire, which is permanently lit making the interior stifling.

Leaning up against the house are several ladders. These are tree trunks with hand holds hewn out of them. They are used to climb on to the roof which is used for water catchment (notice the wooden water spout on the right-hand wall), for grain storage, to provide a cool sleeping area, and for shrines to the spirits of ancestors. The wood in the foreground will be used as fuel. The Lobi do not have the tools capable of preparing the wood as building material. This house is part of a larger settlement of soukalas which are built an arrow's flight (approximately 200 metres) apart.

January is harvest time and to celebrate the gathering of the crops, the children surprise their parents by decorating the outside of their houses. (Similarly, some Christians traditionally decorate their churches at harvest time.) Parents reward children with special treats and gifts.

People have always decorated their homes. Our knowledge of cave-dwellers comes largely from their surviving wall-paintings. House decoration often serves both a practical and an aesthetic function. The paint on a door seals and protects the wood, but the choice of the colour is an outward expression of the owner's taste. Amazonian Indian tribes such as the Barasang sometimes paint their straw or palm walls with ochre, paint and charcoal, depicting the spirit world. Ndebele women of South Africa have turned house decoration into an elaborate art-form. The entire exteriors of their houses are covered in brightly-coloured geometric designs.

People in Britain are generally far more conservative, but they, too, project their images or personalities in the colours they paint their houses or the colours they choose for the roses in their front gardens. British people have not always been so reserved. The Tudors, for example, often adorned their timber-framed houses with brightly coloured patterns influenced by Islamic designs which were popular at the time. Wealthy people decorated their homes with columns or carved patterns, and figures or gargoyles on walls and parapets. Narrowboats display another example of decorative art, the barges showing scenes and wildlife the owners have experienced on their travels along the canals.

DISCUSSION POINTS

1. What would the children expect their parents' response to be if they decorated the outside of their houses as a surprise?
• Discuss what is socially acceptable decoration and what is not, for example graffiti.
• What events do children celebrate that give them the opportunity to decorate their homes. Talk about their experiences of harvest festivals, Diwali, Eid, Christmas and other festivals.

2. What parts of the children's homes are decorated? Help the children to notice the relationship between aesthetic and practical forms of decoration and the purely aesthetic.
• To help children become aware of and develop their personal preferences, ask them to describe what is special about the decoration of their own bedrooms and how their decoration compares with another's choice.

3. Discuss with the children local evidence of people altering the appearance of their homes to make them look different, or individualizing them in some way, for example by painting the brickwork or stone cladding.
• Discuss why people might want to individualize their home in some way.

CLASSROOM ACTIVITIES

ART K.S.1: 1, 5C, 6, 8D, 9C,D,E; K.S.2: 1, 5C, 6, 8D, 9C,D,E.
Lobi children do not have access to ready-made paint or paint brushes. Discuss what they use to decorate their homes. Using natural resources, try creating your own paints by making solutions with crushed clay and chalk for example. Also make a variety of tools for painting.

MATHS K.S.1: UAM 1A; K.S.2: 1A, 3A; SSM 2B, 3A.
The pattern in the picture on the photocard is spots in a row. Using a variety of printed squared and circled paper to help you, design your own repeating patterns. How complex can you make them? Are any of them symmetrical? Can you vary the optical effect through your choice of colour?

ART K.S.1: 1, 2C, 4A, 6, 7A,B,C,D,E,F, 8B,C,D,E,F, 9A,B,D,E; K.S.2: 1, 2C, 4A, 6, 7A,B,C,D,E,F, 8B,C,D,E,F, 9A,B,D,E.
What methods do people use for decorating the interior of their homes? Using interior design books and wallpaper swatches for inspiration, design wallpaper for your home. What would be suitable in rooms such as the bathroom? Combine random and repeating patterns in your designs. Can you think of a quick way of printing your pattern to reproduce it all over a roll of paper?

ART K.S.1: 1, 2C, 4D, 5C, 6, 7A,B,C,D,E,F, 8B,C,D,E,F, 9A,B,D,E; K.S.2: 1, 2C, 4D, 5C, 6, 7A,B,C,D,E,F, 8B,C,D,E,F, 9A,B,D,E.
Lobi houses are large sculptures, modelled from clay. Using red clay, model a similar structure. What difficulties do you encounter? Can you model what you imagine the inside of a Lobi house would be like?

HIST K.S.1: AOS 2; KE 4A; K.S.2: KE 4A.
Reacting to the mass-building of the Industrial Revolution, artists and designers of the nineteenth century included decoration as an integral design feature of objects and buildings. Research people, such as William Morris, who was part of the Arts and Crafts movement in Britain. Are there any buildings of this period in your locality?

43

SCIENCE K.S.1: POS 1b,c, 2a; EIS 1a,b; K.S.2: POS 1b,c, 2a,b; EIS 1a. ART K.S.1: 1, 2b, 4b, 5c, 7e, 8e; K.S.2: 1, 2b, 4b, 5c, 7e, 8e.

Investigate the colours you can make just using the primary colours. Make your own colour chart. Look at colour charts from paint manufacturers. How close can you get to their shades? Make notes on the colours you mix. What do you need to do in order to reproduce a similar colour another time? Look at the names the manufacturers choose for their colours. Can you make up some of your own descriptions? Make up your own words to describe your new colours.

GEO K.S.1: 1a,b, 3b, 5a, 6a,b,c.

Conduct a local street survey to explore ways in which people have 'customized' their homes with the addition of colour, shutters or stick-on stone cladding.

ART K.S.1: 1, 2a,c, 3, 4, 7c,d, 8d,e; K.S.2: 1, 2a,c, 3, 4, 7c,d, 8d,e.

Stick up large sheets of paper on a wall and decorate with whatever pattern you choose. Use a step-ladder to reach the top.

FOLLOW UP WORK

ENG K.S.1 W 1a,b,c; K.S.2: W 1a,b,c.

Invite an interior designer or house-painter into school. Decide what you need to find out and devise a list of questions to support your interview. How will you record the information you receive?

HIST K.S.1: AOS 2; KE 4a,b, 5a; K.S.2: KE 4a,b, 5c. ART: K.S.1: 5b, 7e, 9b,e; K.S.2: 5b, 7e, 9b,e.

In the past wealthy people employed great artists, such as Leonardo da Vinci, to decorate the interior of their homes. Using information books research different fashions in house decoration.

ART. MATHS.

For further work on pattern, look at the pictures of Escher.

BOOKS FOR THE CLASSROOM

MY PAINTED HOUSE, MY FRIENDLY CHICKEN AND ME
by Maya Angelou with photographs by Margaret Courtney-Clarke (Bodley Head 1994)
The life and work of the Ndebele Women in South Africa is captured in exquisite photographs accompanied by a dialogue which explains the decorative crafts a small girl is learning from her mother.

MISERYGUTS
by Morris Gleitzman (Pan Macmillan 1992)
As a surprise birthday present for his dad, Keith decides to paint the outside of their fish and chip shop a tropical mango-orange! This is just one of his ideas to cheer up his mum and dad.

FRIDAY'S RAIN TAKES A LONG TIME TO STOP
by Michael Pennie (Bath College of Higher Education Press 1994)
A 'small book' about African life and art with particular reference to the work of the Lobi people. An entertaining and informative read for adults evoking the atmosphere and character of the places and people encountered by the author.

THE DO-IT-YOURSELF HOUSE THAT JACK BUILT
John Yeoman & Quentin Blake (Puffin 1996)

THE THREE LITTLE WOLVES AND THE BIG BAD DIG
Eugene Trivizas & Helen Oxenbury (Mammoth 1995)

USING THE ACTIVITY SHEET NO: 7

Primarily for children at Key Stage 1, this activity develops and reinforces mathematical reasoning. There is a range of increasingly sophisticated patterns for children to complete, which draw on their skills of recognition and relationships within patterns in order for them to predict what to fill in. They are then given the opportunity to create their own repeating patterns.

PATTERNS

Name.. Class..

HOMES AROUND THE WORLD

■ Look carefully at these patterns. Try to complete them to the end of the row.

■ When you have finished this sheet you could try copying your favourite pattern on to a larger piece of paper. You will need to draw the squares on a larger scale.

■ Try colouring some of them in different shades. Does this alter the pattern you see?

■ Use some of the ideas to create your own patterns in the squares provided.

WAYLAND PUBLISHERS LTD, 61 WESTERN ROAD, HOVE, EAST SUSSEX BN3 1JD

16 MODERN HOUSES SAVE FUEL

AREAS OF STUDY

- Classroom activities and fieldwork exploring questions such as, 'Why is it important to conserve the world's fuel resources, and to restrict pollution?' and 'What can home-owners do to conserve heat energy?'
- An ability to recognize patterns of settlement development in relation to availability of resources, economic activity and human needs.

SKILLS FOR GEOGRAPHY

- Undertake local fieldwork looking at how people can affect their environment.
- Make and use maps and plans.
- Look at ways of sustaining the quality of the environment.
- Consider settlements and land use.

BACKGROUND INFORMATION

In Britain, houses are usually built by large companies or local councils. There is a growing stock of houses and less land available for building. Companies are increasingly reclaiming old buildings for demolition or to conserve and adapt to meet modern standards. The house shown on the photocard is designed to be energy-efficient, using a combination of modern technology and building materials to insulate and heat the house.

The first task at any building site is to survey the land. A professional surveyor marks the boundaries of the building plot and explores the form of the land below and above the surface to record the position of any features that could affect building, such as rock, trees, or natural springs. Measurements are made traditionally using a tape-measure, or by using modern electronic devices. Topographical maps or plans are drawn displaying all the information needed for building construction.

An architect then takes over to design a building that will not collapse and will protect the occupants from the weather and danger from outside. In the past, architects' designs were based on the availability of natural resources. Today's architects have considerably more choice, but the final decisions are ultimately made by the personal preference and budgets of their clients.

Detailed drawings of new buildings are submitted to the local planning office which enforces local regulations governing the style chosen, the height of the finished building, the size of the windows and other such features. Since the Industrial Revolution, housing style has been influenced by the ideas of the Arts and Crafts movement in Britain and the Bauhaus in Germany.

DISCUSSION POINTS

1. Discuss what ideas the children already have for conserving energy in their own home or school, such as turning off lights and closing doors to prevent warm air from escaping.

2. Do the children know of any unusual houses near to them? What makes them different?
- On housing estates, the houses often look very similar. Discuss why, explaining how building costs and functions restrict the design.

3. What materials can the children recognize in the house on the photocard? Why do they think they have been chosen?
- Discuss why the conservation of energy is an integral feature of modern house design.
- Can the children describe how they imagine the inside of this house?
- Encourage children to discuss their likes and dislikes in architectural style.

CLASSROOM ACTIVITIES

IMAGINATIVE PLAY. **GEO KS1: POS 1A,B, 2, 3A,D, 6C: KS2 1B, 2A, 5A, 9B,C, 10A.**	Dampen the sand in the sand-tray and create a landscape with hills, roads and trees. Use toy excavating-vehicles to clear and level the site for building. Consider the best position for building houses. Mark out the plots with sticks and string, and make tracks to show where the roads will go. Decide what facilities you may need in your settlement, such as shops or a playground.

GEO KS1: 1A,B, C,D, 5A, 6A,C; K.S.2: 1A,B, 2A,C, 3A,C. MATHS K.S.1: UAM 1A; SSM 1C, 2A,C, 4A,B; K.S.2: UAM 1A, 2A,B,C,D; SSM 1A,B,E, 2A, 3B,C, 4A,B,C.

Visit your school field or an open space. Investigate its potential as a building site. Measure it. Can you find a way of calculating the elevations of the land? Make a map showing your measurements and locate the position of trees, walls and boundaries.

GEO K.S.1: 1DE, 3C,D; D&T K.S.1: 1B, 2A,C; K.S.2: 1B, 2A,C.

Using Lego, reproduce one floor of your home. Think about the layout of the hall, the lounge, the kitchen, the stairs and so on. Look down on your finished model and draw a plan of what you can see. Take it home to check your accuracy.

ENG KS 1: W 1C; K.S.2: W 1C.

List all the ways your home conserves, or could conserve, energy.

SCIENCE K.S.1: POS 2A,B,C; EIS 1A,B,C, 2A,B,C, 3A,B,C,D,E,F; PP 3A; K.S.2: POS 1A,B,C, 2A,B,C,D, 3A,B; EIS 1A,B,C,D,E, 2A,B,C, 3A,B,C,D,E.

Devise a series of investigations to utilize solar power. How could you heat a small bottle of water using solar power?

GEO K.S.1: 5A, 6A,B; K.S.2: 9A,C. HIST K.S.1: AOS 1B; KE 4A; K.S.2: 4A; SU 3A,D, 3B,C; SU 5A.

Conduct a local street survey to identify differences in architectural design over time.

MATHS K.S.1: SSM 1A, 2A,B,C; K.S.2: SSM 1A,B,E, 2B.

Architectural styles use different shapes and proportions. Design your own style using building blocks and focusing on a particular shape. Can you reproduce your design as a scale drawing?

MATHS K.S.1: SSM 4B; K.S.2: SSM 4A,B,C.

Architects make detailed scale-models showing the inside and outside of a new building. Make your own scale-model of one room.

FOLLOW-UP WORK

ENG K.S.1: W 1A,B,C; K.S.2: W 1A,B,C.

Arrange a visit to your local planning department to find out about the role of a town planner. Perhaps you could view plans and surveys submitted for approval. Alternatively, try to make a similar visit to an architect's office.

ENG K.S.1: W 1A,B,C; K.S.2: W 1A,B,C; K.S.1: SL 1A,B,C,D; 2A; K.S.2: SL 1A,B,C,D; 2A.

After visiting an estate agent's, set up an office in the classroom. Draw a range of houses and write the text for information sheets to sell them. Take clients around imaginary homes and tell them about features.

HIST K.S.1: AOS 1B; KE 4A; K.S.2: 4A; SU 3A,D, 4B,C, 5A.

Many old houses built of brick and stone once belonged to wealthy people. Poorer people's homes were often made of wood and have been replaced. Collect pictures of houses from different architectural periods, and place them on an architectural timeline using information books to help you. Write down your observations of changing styles and building materials. Do you prefer any particular style of architecture?

USING THE ACTIVITY SHEET NO: 8

Rulers, scissors, glue and pencils are needed for this activity. Children are asked to draw the shape of their classroom on the squared grid using a scale of 1 centimetre to represent 1 metre. Symbols in the same scale represent the furniture. This is cut out and used to reproduce a bird's-eye plan of the classroom. Children can rearrange the classroom on paper, and after consultation with the teacher and the whole of the class, put the new layout into practice to provide the most practical working environment.

PLANNING YOUR CLASSROOM

ACTIVITY SHEET 8

Name .... Class ....

- Draw a plan of your classroom on this squared paper.

- Use the scale 1 centimetre to represent 1 metre.

- Remember to label doors, windows, sinks and so on.

- Cut out the symbols to represent the furniture in your classroom. Draw some more if you need to but remember to use the same scale: 1 centimetre to represent 1 metre.

- Do not stick them down until you have checked their position.

- Try rearranging the layout of your classroom. Think about the space needed for lining up at the door, or for access to bookcases or the place where the pencils are kept.

1 metre square table x10

1 metre by ½ metre table x8

computer x1

bookcases x3

storage units x6

teacher's desk x1

carpet x1

WAYLAND PUBLISHERS LTD, 61 WESTERN ROAD, HOVE, EAST SUSSEX BN3 1JD